MEN IN THE KITCHEN

EMMA CROWHURST

KUDOS

First published in Great Britain in 2006 by Kudos, an imprint of Top That! Publishing plc,
Marine House, Tide Mill Way, Woodbridge, Suffolk IP12 1AP, UK
www.kudosbooks.com

0 2 4 6 8 9 7 5 3 1

ISBN 1-84510-882-5

A catalogue record for this book is available from the British Library
Colour reproduction by Reflex Reproduction
Printed and bound in China

Acknowledgments and Credits
Picture credits: Istock, Jo Broome
Managing Director: Barrie Henderson
Kudos Manager: Mike Saiz
Designer: Keely Williams
Senior Editor: Karen Rigden
Junior Editor: Duncan Ballantyne-Way
Photographer Jo Broome
Art Direction: Mike Saiz & Keely Williams

contents

out of the frying pan...

...into the fire?

Does the world really need another cookbook? There are so many already, on so many subjects. Hundreds of mouth-watering recipes, masses of information, all to inspire and encourage the cook. However, if you've never set foot in a kitchen except to place your cup on the draining board or to get another beer from the fridge, then these books, packed with techniques and ingredients, may as well be in a foreign language. When I used to teach cooking, it was the complete beginner that gave me the most pleasure – the person who at first needed to be coaxed into their apron and shown the difference between a measuring jug and a lemon squeezer. Folk who had literally never cooked in their life. It just so happens that many of those individuals were men.

The excitement and satisfaction of eating something delicious and home-made for the first time when you've never cooked before is unsurpassed and impossible for the experienced cook to envisage.

Countless male chefs appear on the television and you would think that this would motivate men to get in there and cook, but the flash world of TV cooking can instil the fear of God into any of us, male or female.

This book is for the man who struggles with even the idea of scrambled egg, or wrestles with roast dinner only to find the roast dinner wins! I want to get more men into the kitchen. All those who say they wouldn't know where to begin, come this way and let me provide a fundamental and basic view into the kitchen, its necessary equipment, choosing and buying ingredients and an essential collection of easy-to-follow recipes which will carry you through to becoming a competent, amateur cook. Very few people are born with the ability to be organised enough to cook but it can be learnt. With some expert tips and advice you can gain confidence and experience the pleasure of eating non-processed, healthy and delicious food. This is a simple book and does not pretend to be a heavyweight. Think of it as an introduction to the pleasure of cooking. Above all cooking should be relaxing and enjoyable.

kitchen essentials

Most labour-saving devices are unnecessary for the very basic cook. Whether you are cooking in a caravan or a castle, the requirements are pretty much the same.

You can use this chapter to help you begin kitting out your kitchen or simply to add a few essentials.

Knives

The most basic item of equipment has to be knives. Kitchen knives must be a good weight, so don't go for the cheapest plastic handles, you need to be able to sharpen them. The top three are:
- A medium-sized cook's knife, with a slightly curved blade for chopping vegetables
- A small knife, sometimes called an office or paring knife
- A serrated or bread knife

An additional knife that can be useful is the palette knife, for turning food in a hot pan.

Knife sharpening

There are many ways to sharpen knives, including electrical gadgets but I prefer to use a steel, which is a standard chef's tool for sharpening. To use a steel, stand the point on a

A cook's knife

Paring knife

Bread knife

Palette knife

Knife-sharpening steel

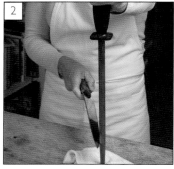

chopping board, the tip in a cloth to keep it in place. Draw the knife down the steel from handle to tip at a 45° angle. Do this on both sides of the blade evenly and test the knife carefully with your thumb, repeating the process until the blade is sharp. Always wipe the knife after sharpening to remove any metal filings.

Do take care with sharpening, if you get it wrong you may blunt the knives. If in any doubt, you can take them to a shoe repair shop – they will usually sharpen knives for a small fee per knife. Finally, do not try to sharpen serrated knives as this will ruin them.

Chopping boards

You need to have at least two chopping boards. They should be made of wood or plastic and be thick and totally flat. They should not wobble when you are chopping and it helps to place a clean, damp cloth underneath to stop it moving while you are cutting.

To clean your chopping board, rinse it first under cold water to wash away meat or food juices and to prevent them 'cooking' into the board. Then scrub with hot soapy water and a stiff washing up brush, rinse with clean water and dry well. Stand on its end and allow ventilation space. It is often easiest – and safest – to have one board for raw meat and fish and one for cooked food; catch up on this in the health and safety chapter later (see page 46).

Chopping boards

Bowls

Metal, glass and plastic are useful, so if possible have some of each. Glass and metal are easy to wash. If you go for plastic, make sure you wash the bowl really well as plastic can easily be tainted by strong tastes and colours, for example beef chilli. Metal bowls are not recommended for acidic sauces containing lime or lemon juice (they can add a metallic aftertaste), so use glass for those recipes. Similarly, metal spoons should be avoided for the same foodstuffs, opt for wooden ones instead. The last consideration is that glass and plastic can be microwaved. Skim over any recipe first to check how the bowl and its contents are to be used.

Pots & pans

Metal, heavy-based pans are superb for most types of hob cooking and if you get ones that can also go in the oven you save on cupboard space. One or two non-stick saucepans; a griddle pan (pictured middle right) and a medium-sized, non-stick frying pan should cover you for most things. As you expand your collection copper pots are a useful addition as, unlike conventional pans, they distribute the heat evenly – particularly important when making a delicate sauce that might catch (burn) easily. With all pans remember to use an oven mitt or pot holder if the handle isn't insulated.

Glass and metal bowls

Pots and pans

Wok

If you're a fan of stir fries then you'll find a wok indispensable. With either a slightly flat, or rounded bottom (for use over gas burners), all woks are circular with high sides for fast, high-heat cooking. Choose between a non-stick or carbon steel model but bear in mind that the constant stirring and scrapping can remove the teflon coating on non-stick woks.

Wok

Baking & cake tins

Roasting and baking both sweet and savoury items requires a few essential items. Make sure you have a non-stick baking sheet, a roasting/baking tin with approximately one inch-high sides and also a cake tin or sandwich cake tins. I use two 20 cm sandwich tins later (page 132) but if you prefer you could buy one deep tin, about 8 cm deep. There are several styles of deep tin to choose from, for a beginner I'd recommend one with a detachable base with a clip on the side of the tin which makes removing the cake easier.

Baking & cake tins

Pastry cutters

Pastry and cookie cutters are also useful items to have. As well as using them for cutting pastry or biscuits, I often use them when cooking patties such as the Thai fish cakes (page 90) or burgers (page 55) and for shaping desserts such as cheesecakes (page 131).

Pastry cutters

A vegetable peeler

A sharp paring knife can be used to peel fruit and vegetables but a peeler is much easier to handle. The one I prefer is the wide, swivel-head peeler.

A vegetable peeler

Whisks

Balloon (left) or coiled whisks (right) are used for mixing batters, sauces and cake mixes and for beating eggs. Electric whisks can be used for more time consuming jobs, such as whisking egg whites for meringues (see page 127).

WIre whisks

Kitchen scissors

Buy them from a cook shop and keep them just for cooking. Good for cutting up sausages, trimming chicken and snipping bacon and herbs.

Kitchen scissors

Fish slice

A slim one is best but a palette knife will do the same job, which is basically turning delicate food over while frying or grilling. Fish slices also come in handy for stir fries or stirring thick sauces.

Fish slice

Piping bag

A piping bag, and various nozzles, isn't an essential item in your kitchen but I have used one to add mash potato to the fish pie on page 95. They can also be used to pipe cream or icing. Your early attempts may look a bit messy, but just try to apply constant pressure and remember, practise makes perfect.

Piping bag

Kitchen tongs

If you've always insisted in being in charge of the barbecue then you may already be familiar with this tool. Tongs are perfect for grabbing food, turning stuff over, such as sausages, and serving up.

Perforated/slotted spoon

For draining vegetables, general stirring and serving up. Just watch out for the hot water and juices dripping through.

Wooden spoons

You want to have about five of these in different sizes and include a straight-edged spatula in your collection. They are good for all stirring, especially in non-stick pans.

Ladle

This is basically a small bowl with a handle for serving soup, stews and sauces.

Sieves & colanders

These are good for straining cooked vegetables, rice and pasta and, of course, sieving flours. Make sure your sieve is completely dry before sifting flour. Large portions of vegetables, rice or pasta can be more easily drained with a colander. Essentially the same as a sieve, although bigger, colanders generally have two handles and often have a base so it can stand in the sink as you use it.

Measuring equipment

A measuring jug is essential; choose glass or plastic, whichever you prefer. You will also need scales. Electric ones are great, as ounces and grams can be measured accurately. Measuring spoons are really useful for tablespoon and teaspoon measures, I prefer stainless steel spoons.

Serving plates

Large white plates are excellent for all types of food. Go for all the same style in large and medium. For my starters and puddings I actually use medium-sized plates, which are an average main course size. The very large plates (32 cm/12 in.) I use for main courses. Big plates make the food look so much better and the space on the plate helps to show the food off (see the section on presentation, pages 48–49).

A box grater & hand-held grater

A box grater is perfect for cheese and vegetables. It has four sides, hence the name, and each side has different sized grating holes. Hand-held utensils are more convenient for grating small amounts, for example nutmeg or Parmesan cheese.

Zester

Great for removing the zest of citrus fruit in delicate strands and a lot kinder on your knuckles as well, but not essential.

Measuring equipment

Serving plates

Zester, box grater & hand-held grater.

turning up the heat

Gas or electricity ?

Once you have the basic equipment you are nearly ready to cook. But before we look at the food, what will you actually be cooking on?

Gas is instant and usually lights with an ignition button. It may take a bit of getting used to. The flames must not lick up around the pan (it's an expensive waste of resources and could burn you or the pan) so use the right-sized flame for the size of pan.

Electricity is easy to turn on and control but just like gas you have to get used to your particular oven. You need to be aware when boiling things on an electric hob that it doesn't respond as instantly as gas.

The kinds of things you do on a hob include all the stages of heating different liquids, from poaching – the most gentle – through simmering and on to boiling, which is the fiercest, as well as steaming, where water is boiled but the food is held above the water, cooking in the steam. The addition of some kind of fat (butter, oil etc) to the pan lets you sweat, sauté, fry, griddle, stir-fry and pan-fry on the hob.

In the oven you can roast, bake, braise, brown and casserole. Many ovens these days have the grill inside and this means you cannot use the oven and grill at the same time.

microwave cooking

one of the easiest places to bake a potato

The microwave – a common but under-used tool in most kitchens – is usually only used for reheating and defrosting. However, all manner of things can be cooked in the microwave, from soup to Christmas cake. To list the full potential of a microwave is another book for another day, but if you have a microwave, do read the booklet that comes with it as it will have all kinds of quick ideas you may like to try.

Jacket potatoes

The easiest thing to cook in the microwave is a jacket potato. Take a 170 g/6 oz potato, wash it and pierce the skin with a fork. Stand on a plate and microwave on full power for six minutes. Turn the potato during the cooking once or twice. Be careful – of course – as it gets hot. Test the potato with a cutlery knife to see if it's tender. Give it an extra minute if necessary and check again. The potato will not have the oven crisp skin but is fine as a quick snack for one person. If you have a little more time, place the potato in a hot oven for about 15 minutes to crisp up the skin.

scrambled eggs

Another good microwave quickie is scrambled eggs. For one person: beat one egg thoroughly with two teaspoons of milk and season with salt and pepper. Pour into a buttered mug, cover with a saucer and cook on full power for 30 seconds. Remove from the microwave and stir with a fork, cover and cook on full for another 15 seconds until the egg is lightly set. Stir again and eat at once. Don't cook the egg more than this or omit the stirring after 30 seconds or you'll end up with a rubbery and inedible mess. There are other egg dishes that can be cooked in the microwave, again check out the instruction book, but eggs in their shell will explode in the microwave and make a terrible mess.

I will say more on microwave cooking in the vegetable section (page 23) but as a general tip; baked beans, soups and sauces should be covered with pierced clingfilm as they can also make an awful mess. Accidents will happen though and to clean any dried on food either mix a cup of water with a cup of white vinegar, or use a cup of water and two tablespoons of baking soda and another two of lemon juice, stick it in the microwave to boil and steam, then just wipe the inside clean with kitchen roll.

getting stocked up

it's time to hit the shops

Food shopping should never be done on an empty stomach. The reason is obvious as it will cause you to stock up on all kinds of things that you don't really need.

Make a list if you can and try to stick to it, but observe any special offers or three-for-two type deals – if they were things you would have wanted anyway.

The supermarket is the easiest choice for many people but it is killing independent small shops. Try to visit local stores such as the butcher, the greengrocer and a fishmonger if you can find one. All the food will be fresher and more seasonal and – almost as important – more local. The store cupboard is the backbone of the kitchen and a well-stocked one will allow you to make most dishes without having to make a special trip to the shops. See the helpful list in the store cupboard section (pages 38-44).

vegetables

are a good source of vitamins and minerals

It is recommended that we eat at least five portions of fruit and vegetables a day. Vegetables such as potatoes, sweet potatoes, parsnips, swedes and turnips contain starch and sugar for energy. Green vegetables such as spinach and broccoli are a good source of vitamins and minerals. However, these vitamins are water-soluble so careful cooking and preparation are vital to preserve their goodness.

When choosing vegetables, look for unblemished leaves or skin, and root vegetables, such as carrots and potatoes, should be firm to the touch. As far as portions go, weigh your vegetables before cooking; the combined weight of all the vegetables that you are preparing should be 110 g/4 oz per person. Once you become more familiar and confident you will find that you no longer need to weigh them, but can rely on your own judgement.

Buying organic

The most important issue with cooking should be the taste. That is, after all, the point. Food produced naturally and in season will always have a better flavour and more nutrients than crops that have been sprayed and cultivated out of season.

Try to buy organic fruit and vegetables whenever you can, the more people buy them the cheaper they will get and although their shelf life is shorter than the standard supermarket produce; it should discipline you to use it up and shop more often. An organic weekly delivery such as those some farm shops offer is a good way to get into it. Buying fresh often makes you plan your weekly meals around what you have, using whatever is left at the end of the week to make a delicious soup. If you're still not convinced, read my section on going organic on page 45.

preparing your veggies

Many will already be familiar with how to prepare their vegetables but for those of you who need that extra bit of guidance, or maybe just some reassurance, read on.

Storage

Fruit and vegetables kept in plastic bags or covered in clingfilm in the supermarket will become damp and slimy if left in their packaging. So remove any packaging when you unpack your shopping, and store in a cool ventilated place. A vegetable rack in a very cool place is ideal although you can also use the bottom of the fridge. Just make sure you rotate your shopping and don't just chuck the new veg on top of the old. Salad items should be stored in the fridge and used within a few days.

Preparation

All vegetables should be washed before use, even if they are to be peeled. Only fruit and vegetables that discolour (such as apples and potatoes) need to go into water before cooking. However, if you intend to roast or caramelise them then any browning won't matter.

Broccoli & cauliflower

These two vegetables can be cut into florets (little bunches) with the stalk left on. They do not need to go into water until you are ready to cook. Cut along the natural divisions of the stalks just above where they meet the main stalk (1 & 2). If you have a particularly large floret, split it by first cutting the stalk slightly then gently prise apart with your fingers (3).

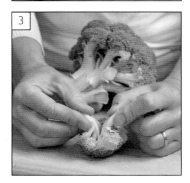

give your vegetables a good clean first

Cabbage

To prepare cabbage, especially loose-leaved cabbages such as savoys, cut the head into quarters and remove the stalk (1). Rest a flat edge of the cabbage on the board and cut into fine strips (2). Separate the strips, which can trap dirt, and rinse well under running water before continuing to cook your cabbage as preferred. With the larger, outer leaves it may be easier to use an alternative method. With a single, whole leaf make two cuts to remove the stalky part of the leaf (3 & 4). Repeat with a few more leaves then roll them up together to form a bundle (5), then, as before, cut fine strips working along the length of the bundle (6). Don't forget to rinse the cabbage thoroughly.

Carrots

These should be washed, peeled and cut into rounds or batons and stored out of water, but covered before use. Rounds should be cut in straight even sections, roughly 5 mm thick (7), although if you were adding carrot to a stew you may prefer to slice more robust pieces. Batons are simply sticks of carrot. Begin by cutting your carrot into 5 cm lengths (8). Then, watching your fingers, slice down the

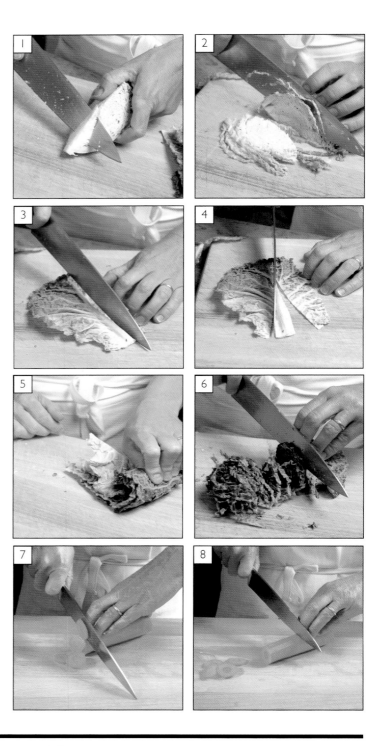

carrot to form wide strips, about four strips although it depends on the size of your carrot (9). Pile about three slices on top of each other then cut the strips into sticks (10). Cutting thin batons is known as cutting julienne.

Leeks

Being a root vegetable, leeks are often very dirty so make one slit down to the middle, but not through to the other side (11) then rinse under cold water loosening the leaves slightly. The leek can then be finely chopped (12). Alternatively, cut them into rounds or long strips and wash well before cooking (13).

Potatoes

The preparation of your potatoes depends on your final dish. In all cases though they must be thoroughly washed. Jacket potatoes can then be cooked directly, as can new potatoes either by boiling or try baking them, see page 116. Roast (page 68), mashed (page 94) or boiled potatoes need to be peeled and cut into large even-sized pieces (14). Store in cold water if you are not cooking straight away. Other dishes may call for thin rounds of potato (15), for example Lancashire hotpot, or thick batons or wedges (16) for chips (page 114) – in these instances cut in the same way as for a carrot but adjust the thickness accordingly.

Salad leaves

All salad leaves should be gently washed before use and then torn or cut into pieces. To remove excess water spin in a salad spinner (1) or wrap the leaves in a clean tea towel and take into the garden for a good shake – make sure the leaves stay wrapped up.

Spinach

Spinach makes a great addition to a salad but whether cooking it or eating it raw, it should be washed at least three times to get all the dirt out. Drain well before cooking.

To slice an onion

Using a sharp knife cut the top off the onion (2). Place on its flat end and cut in half through the root (3). Peel each half and discard the skin (4). With the root towards your left (right-handers) cut thin half circles from the onion (5). Keep cutting until you get close to the root.

To finely chop an onion

Cut the onion in half and peel as before. With the cut side down, make a horizontal cut about halfway up cutting towards but stopping short of the root. Then make about six downward slits, beginning at the top of the onion close to the root (6). The rest of the onion is cut as though slicing it but you should have neat little cubes (7 & 8). The more horizontal and vertical cuts made, the finer the onion will be chopped.

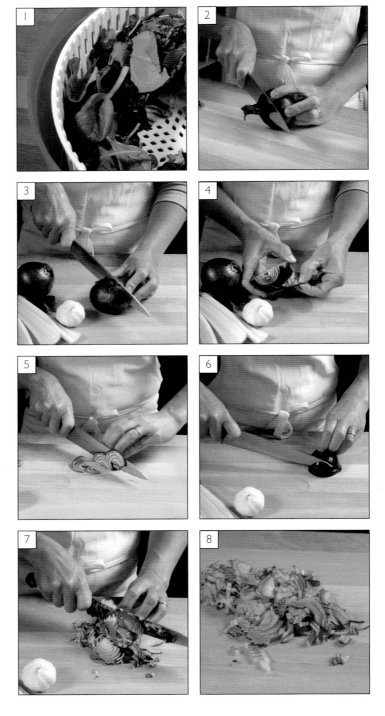

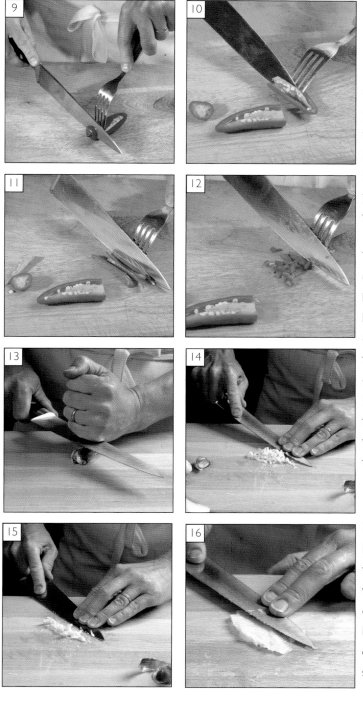

Chillies

Chillies are very hot and when preparing them you need to take care: either wear gloves or hold with a fork while cutting. Keep your head well back in case any juice spits up and wash your hands thoroughly after handling. Don't touch your eyes during or immediately after handling the chillies.

To finely dice a fresh chilli, firstly remove the top using a sharp knife and fork (9). Slice in half horizontally and remove the seeds (10). Cutting lengthways, you can then cut the first half of the chilli into thin strips (11), bundle these strips together and cut across the strips to create small dice (12). Repeat with the second half of the chilli if needed. A note about seeds: these don't have to be removed if you and your guests can take the heat. If you do want a hotter dish simply leave the seeds in.

Crushing garlic

Break the head of garlic into cloves and using a large knife, with the blade away from you, crush the clove by pressing down firmly on the knife with your fist (13). The papery skin should now come off easily. Cut the root piece and discard. Roughly chop the clove and use the knife to crush the pieces against the board (14–16). Using salt acts as an abrasive to help with the crushing.

cooking vegetables

There are a number of ways to cook vegetables from roasting to stir-frying, to steaming and boiling. Modern tastes and my own are not to over cook vegetables and serve them (unless a starchy root vegetable) with some crunch, otherwise known as *al denté*. Most of the times and methods I've given will cook to *al denté*. Should you prefer your vegetables softer than this then cook them for a bit longer but check them regularly.

General vegetable cooking

Potatoes go into cold salted water. Bring them up to the boil and simmer with a lid until tender – this usually takes about 30 minutes from cold; test with a cutlery knife. It should penetrate easily. New potatoes go into salted boiling water and don't need so long.

Batons or rounds of *carrot* can go into boiling salted water or be steamed. Cook with a lid for 3–5 minutes. I like my carrots quite firm with a little crunch but if you prefer them otherwise just cook them for longer.

Broccoli cooks in the same way as carrots but for about 2 minutes. Do not over cook as it goes a horrid khaki colour and starts to flop. *Leeks* take a little longer and should not be served too crunchy.

Exact cooking times are difficult to predict as it depends on how thick or small the vegetables are cut. The best way to become familiar with cooking times is to test the veg after two minutes and then each minute thereafter.

Boiling

Boiling involves placing vegetables into just enough boiling, salted water to cover the vegetables, or placing them in cold water and bringing to the boil. Covering with a lid speeds up the cooking time and saves energy by not losing heat. Boil each type of vegetable separately. Green vegetables and carrots are usually served *al denté*. Root vegetables are usually served tender, so they can be mashed. In

general, root vegetables go into cold water, and are brought up to the boil and then simmered until cooked. Green vegetables generally go into boiling water. However, this is not always so and smaller cuts of root vegetables – such as carrots and new potatoes – should be placed in boiling water.

Steaming

Steaming is done by putting a pan of boiling water beneath another pan with holes (similar to a metal colander) to let the steam through. It should be an exact fit and should have a tight fitting lid. Most steamers are sold with one or two layers. Steaming is the healthiest way to cook vegetables, as fewer vitamins and minerals are lost to the water. All vegetables are cooked for the minimum time to reduce the loss of nutrients. If you have the space and do a lot of steaming then an electric steamer (above) is a good investment, follow the manufacturer's

instructions for use. Bamboo steamers (below) are a good option if you can find one to exactly fit one of your pans. They often have three layers and so save on hob space. You can also buy microwave steamers, but I don't tend to cook any vegetables in the microwave as this can destroy the vitamins and nutrients. However, if you suddenly find yourself caught short and needing veg in a hurry, it is always an option. As a general rule, place your veg in a non metallic bowl or microwave steamer with a couple of tablespoons of water, and microwave on full power for a few minutes at a time (or follow the manufacturer's instructions), checking to see whether the vegetables are done. Always allow to stand for a minute as cooking continues after the microwave has stopped.

Stir-frying

Stir-frying is a quick cooking method, which suits vegetables that can be served with crunch such as, carrots, sweet peppers, mushrooms, bean sprouts, baby corn, French beans, mange tout, spring onions and celery. Cut the larger vegetables as thinly as you can and heat a small amount of oil in a wok or large pan. Wait until the oil is very hot and start by adding some crushed garlic and maybe some grated ginger. Then add the vegetables, starting with the firmest first. Keep them moving in the pan ('stir' frying) and cook until all are just beginning to soften but still have some bite, always add the bean sprouts last. You may finish with soy sauce and a little sesame oil.

Roasting

Roasted vegetables are normally just reserved for Sunday lunch and few people look beyond the potato, or maybe the odd parsnip. In fact there are a number of vegetables that can be roasted which, when cooked in this way produce the most intense flavours. For the modern cook though the real value to roasting as a cooking method is the ease and simplicity of it, and while they cook you're free to take on other kitchen tasks. It could hardly be easier to chop a few vegetables and place them in a roasting tray with oil and seasoning, then just bung them in the oven, essentially that's all there is to it. If you don't believe me then try out the recipe on page 118.

Blanching

For a dinner party or a busy cooking session, I cook and blanch my veg. This means I slightly under cook the vegetables and then plunge them into very cold water, changing the water a few times so the vegetables cool in the fastest possible time. Then drain and dry well. The vegetables can then be stored in the fridge until later. The vegetables can then be re-heated in the microwave until piping hot or plunged back into boiling water at the last minute. You will lose some of the vegetables' vitamins by cooking them this way but if you are stuck for time and space this method will take off some of the pressure.

meat

When choosing meat the recipe will usually specify exactly what sort of cut or type of meat to buy. It can be daunting to go to a meat counter and have to ask for something, especially when you haven't a clue what it should look like. Using a good butcher is my main recommendation; they can tell you all about cuts of meat and what they should be used for — remember it's part of their job to offer advice and assistance.

which meat, what for and how to cook it

Tough & tender

There are several factors that affect the tenderness of a piece of meat. The age of the animal must be taken into account. The younger the animal the less exercise it will have taken and therefore the more tender its meat will be.

The other main factor is where on the animal the meat is taken from. The parts of the body that do the most work, such as the legs, neck and shoulders, will be tougher and have more connective tissue (which is the name for the structures that support muscles in meat). In culinary terms, the more connective tissue a piece of meat has, the longer and slower the cooking time required. These tougher cuts of meat can be cooked in ways to soften the connective tissue, so that it is not obvious when you eat the meat. When connective tissue breaks down it releases gelatin, which gives soft, sticky tenderness. Long, slow, gentle cooking will break down the connective tissue leaving a butter-soft consistency to the meat. It is this softening of connective tissue that gives a casserole its richness. Another benefit is usually a rich delicious sauce which needs little or no finishing. It is generally considered that the tougher cuts of meat have more flavour.

A common mistake people make, is to think that a casserole would be even better with an expensive cut of meat, but as these more pricey cuts have far less connective tissue, the slow cooking process means that they simply dry out and are fibrous.

Perfect methods of cooking for usually tough cuts of meat are braising, casseroling, pot roasting and stewing. All are moist methods that involve browning the meat and then adding flavoured liquid such as stock, wine or beer and then cooking slowly in a heavy pan on the hob or in the oven.

For the cuts of meat that do not work hard in the animal, the cooking methods are quicker and usually dry, so not in liquid. Grilling, griddling, and frying are typical ways to cook tender cuts of meat. Roasting is also used for the larger tender cuts.

Definitions of the cooking methods

The following terms are often found in cookery books and can be confusing.

Stewing — To cook very slowly in a covered pan with liquid in the oven or on the hob.

Braising — To stew with vegetables in a covered pan in the oven.

Casseroling — Same as the above but in a casserole dish with a lid in the oven or on the hob.

Roasting — To cook in the oven uncovered usually without liquid, but with some basting.

Pot roasted — To cook in a pot to encourage a moist environment in the oven or on the hob.

Frying — A fierce, stove-top heat cooked with oil or fat.

Grilling — Cooked under a preheated grill.

Griddling — Using a ribbed pan over a fierce, stove-top heat. (Benefits are being able to use less oil and having a ribbed pattern on the meat.)

beef

There are around 60 cuts of beef, many with different names — so don't worry if you get confused. Tender cuts of beef are rib, sirloin, fillet and rump (slightly tougher but still considered to be a tender cut). Tough cuts are the shoulders, legs and neck. Here is a simple run down of methods of cooking and suitable cuts of meat.

Braising, stewing
and casseroling — Shin, chuck steak, brisket, flank and neck.
Meat labelled for these methods (e.g. 'stewing steak') often will not specify exactly which tougher cut it is.

Roasting — Fore rib, sirloin, fillet (butchers also recommend topside).

Frying, grilling
and griddling — Rump steak, sirloin steak, fillet steak, rib-eye and t-bone steak.

Pot roasting — Topside, silverside.

Cuts of Beef

NECK | CHUCK AND BLADE | FORE RIB | SIRLOIN | RUMP | TOPSIDE SILVERSIDE
CLOD | THICK RIB | THIN RIB | HINDQUARTER FLANK | THICK FLANK | LEG
SHIN | BRISKET

Steak

Learning how to cook steak is a trial and error process. Begin with a nice thick sirloin steak and cut it as you cook it to see what is happening inside. Heat a half tablespoon of oil in a heavy pan, allow it to smoke slightly, and place in the steak, seasoned with salt and pepper. Cook for two minutes each side and then cut a slice off to see what the inside is like. Return it to the pan and continue cooking for another two minutes, etc. Another trick to gauge how your steak is cooking is to compare the feel of the meat to the fleshly pad beneath your thumb as you bring your thumb and index finger together, then your thumb and middle finger and so on. You should notice that the pad feels really squishy at first then becomes firmer as you bring the other fingers together; your thumb and index finger feels similar to a rare steak and so on. All the quick cooked steaks are better served rare or medium rare, once the fibres are completely cooked all moisture is gone from the meat and with the moisture goes the tenderness.

How cooked is your steak?

rare
Definition -
Hot and bloody but no fibres showing in the middle

medium
Definition -
Very hot and pink, some cooked fibres

well done
Definition -
Extremely hot and almost no pink, fibres completely cooked

lamb

The same tough and tender rules apply to lamb as to beef. Animals which weigh more than 36 kg/80 lb are considered to be mutton, and are generally older sheep. However, mutton is increasingly difficult to find these days – which is a shame as it is very tasty, following the rule of tougher meat giving more flavour. Less than 36 kg and the meat is considered lamb, however there is a difference between new season lamb and older, larger lambs that are killed later in the year. The younger the lamb, the sweeter and more tender the flesh. Almost all cuts are suitable for grilling, frying and roasting. The fattier, cheaper cuts are better for casseroles. Lamb should be brownish pink when cooked.

Roasting –	Leg, shoulder, saddle, best end of neck, loin or breast.
Braising –	Chump chops, shoulder or leg.
Grilling, griddling and frying –	Best end cutlets, loin chops, and fillet steaks.
Casseroles and stewing –	Knuckle, shanks scrag and middle neck.

chicken

Taste tests have been done with free range and battery-farmed chickens and the free range is always the winner. Although more expensive I think it is absolutely worth the money. Chicken should always be tender and, as long as you do not over cook it, it will be delicious. One large chicken should serve four people.

Cutting your chicken

When cutting a raw chicken for a casserole remove the breasts and cut each into two. Remove the legs and divide the thigh and drumstick. You can buy them already cut, but usually drumsticks, thighs and breasts are sold separately.

Breasts are perfect for barbecues, roasting, grilling and frying, but always check they are cooked through (very hot and firm to the touch with no pink flesh). If you are including breasts in a casserole avoid over cooking them and add them later on in the cooking time. They will not be as succulent or as tender in a casserole. The legs and thighs are more forgiving and are perfect for casseroles and braised dishes.

pork

The raw flesh should be pale pink and not red or bloody. Pork is generally killed young for the fresh meat market and so is quite tender. The fat and skin are usually removed before cooking except when roasting, when they make good crackling.

Crackling

To make great crackling you must score the skin with a very sharp knife, through the fat but not to the flesh. Brush with oil and rub on plenty of salt. Roast at a high temperature (220°C/425°F/gas mark 7) for at least 30 minutes with the fat side uppermost. Once the crackling has formed turn the oven down to 190°C/375°F/gas mark 5 for the rest of the cooking time (see table).

roasts

To calculate cooking times of any meat you need to weigh it and then you can use this table to calculate how it should be cooked. All meats need a good 20 minutes start before you apply the formula (see below). Always preheat the oven and cook for the required time – don't be tempted to turn the oven up and reduce the cooking time, you'll simply have a burnt outside and raw inner meat. To test the meat you can insert a metal skewer into the thickest part and leave for 15 seconds. Then remove and briefly test on the back of your hand – if the skewer is very hot the meat is cooked, alternatively use a thermometer and refer to the figures below. When cooking chicken, the juices will run clear once the bird is cooked.

MEAT	TEMPERATURE			COOKING TIME		TEMPERATURE ON THERMOMETER
	°C	°F	gas mark	per kg	per lb	
BEEF						
To start	220	425	7	20 mins		
Rare roast	160	320	3	35 mins	15 mins	60°C/140°F
Medium roast	160	320	3	45 mins	20 mins	70°C/158°F
Well done	160	320	3	55 mins	25 mins	80°C/176°F
PORK						
To start	220	425	7	30 mins		
Down to	200	400	6	65 mins	25mins	80°C/176°F
LAMB						
To start	200	400	6	20 mins +		
Down to	190	375	5	55 mins	20 mins	70°C/158°F
CHICKEN	NB: however small the chicken, it usually takes at least an hour to cook					
To start	200	400	6	20 mins		
Roast	200	400	6	35-40	15-20	80°C/176°F

fish

Knowing how to prepare and cook fish, and which fish to use for which recipes is a tricky business. The feel of the cold, wet fish can be off-putting to some, but the flavour and texture of well-cooked seafood is a delight.

Luckily the preparation of fish can be taken care of by your fishmonger, but it is good to know exactly how it should be prepared for certain recipes; for example, you don't want a trout filleted if you are cooking it whole on the barbecue.

well-cooked seafood is a delight!

To choose your fish you first need to know if it is fresh. Look for:

- Bright eyes that are not sunken and cloudy
- Firm flesh
- A fresh seaside smell; if your fish pongs it is not fresh
- Scales should not be falling off
- Not too much flexibility

The fishmonger can gut, remove fins, gills and scales, fillet and skin the fish, all to suit your requirements, most recipes will tell you what to ask for. Some fish will need pin boning (the very tiny bones in trout and other round fish) – this the fishmonger won't do, so a small pair of pliers or tweezers are a great help. Having said that, the small bones are good for you and can be eaten.

Fish is a valuable source of protein, vitamin D (in oily fish) and most contain little fat. They are categorised in several ways; white or oily; or round or flat.

Oily fish have the oil dispersed throughout the flesh, whereas white fish have the oil concentrated in their liver. Flat fish have four fillets and do not have large scales – examples are: sole, brill, turbot, plaice and halibut. Round fish have two fillets and the larger fish can have annoying scales – examples are: salmon, trout, cod, whiting, sardines, mackerel and red snapper.

If you are going to prepare your own fish you need a fish knife. This is a very sharp, flexible knife that is perfect for taking the fish off the bones and skinning. Use the back of the knife for removing the scales, and scissors for removing fins and gills.

Cuts of fish

A fillet

A loin of cod

A steak on the bone

Fish substitutions

Fish and seafood are regional and seasonal, so the type specified in a recipe may not always be available. Here fish and seafood are grouped with their most suitable substitutes:

- Sole, brill, flounder
- Brill, turbot, John Dory
- Cod, haddock, halibut, hake, monkfish, coley
- Red snapper, red mullet, grouper
- Tuna, swordfish, shark
- Mackerel, herring, sardines
- Seabass, salmon (especially steaks and fillets)
- Mussels, clams
- King prawn, monkfish

Shellfish

There are two main types of shellfish – the crustaceans: lobsters, crabs, prawns, shrimps; and molluscs: single-shell creatures such as whelks and winkles, two-shell or bi-valve creatures such as clams, oysters, mussels and scallops, and creatures with a kind of internal shell such as squid and octopus.

Lobsters and crabs can be placed into hot water and then gently poached. For lobster allow eight minutes for every 450 g/1 lb; for crab 15 minutes for every 450 g /1 lb. Both can be bought precooked and the crab is often completely prepared and sold as dressed crab. Prawns can be bought raw (often frozen) when they are a grey/blue colour. They can also be purchased cooked (also often frozen), when they will be the bright pinky red that you associate with cooked shellfish. Prawns are sold shell on or shell off (peeled), but it is an easy job to remove the head, tail and legs.

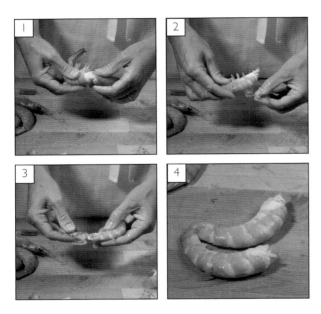

To shell prawns

Pull off the prawn's head and with your thumb positioned under the legs (1). Then unwrap the shell from around the tail and the legs should come off with the shell on the back (2). Then just gently pull off the final tailpiece (3).

shellfish & safety

It is vital that all shellfish be fresh, otherwise serious food poisoning can occur. Make sure you buy it either live, frozen or just cooked. Fresh mussels should be closed and unbroken. If they are a little open you can check if they are still alive by tapping them, if they are alive and still safe to eat they will close, if they don't they are dead

and should be thrown away. Before cooking you need to use a sharp knife to scrape the shells and remove the barnacles and hairy thread called the beard.

Cooking fish

Like meat, fish is made up of muscle fibres that vary in length. The fibres have very little connective tissue and this breaks down very easily during cooking. It is easy to over cook fish, resulting in it falling apart and becoming dry. Some fish do not have a very strong flavour and so simplicity and quick cooking is recommended. Fish should be the main event, rather than placing too many complicated flavours together.

How do you tell if fish is cooked?

Raw fish is translucent and glassy looking. As it cooks it quickly becomes opaque. When it is hot through to the centre, it will be cooked. The perfectly cooked piece of fish is just turning from translucent to opaque.

When learning to cook anything, it is a case of trial and error. Why not cook an extra piece of fish so you can cut it and pierce with a skewer to see whether it is cooked? To test the fish, insert a metal skewer into the thickest part and leave for 15 seconds. Then remove and test on the back of your hand. Do this quickly – if the skewer is very hot (too hot to hold against your hand) the fish is cooked. Salmon is often served a little underdone, slightly glassy in the centre but still hot. Tuna can be served rare when it has a butter-soft texture; if tuna is allowed to cook fully through it will be dry and fibrous. Some people prefer it that way, as they do with a well-done steak. It is often all about personal taste.

Ways of cooking fish

All fish should be seasoned with salt and pepper prior to cooking, and served as soon as it is cooked, unless the fish is to be flaked into a salad and served cold, for example a fresh tuna salad.

Steaming

Steaming is a great way to cook fish as many of the vitamins – and indeed aspects of the flavour – are water-soluble; by steaming you won't lose anything to the liquid. Try it in a steamer, or wrapped in leaves such as spinach or banana leaves.

Poaching

Poaching means cooking gently in barely bubbling liquid. This could be water flavoured with peppercorns, bay leaves and a little vinegar or milk, as in a fish pie (see page 93), where the liquid is used for the sauce.

Griddling

This is much the same as pan frying but uses oil not butter. The griddle pan must be almost smoking hot. Use firm steaks or fillets, as the fish is liable to break up. These tips also apply if you are barbecuing your fish.

Pan frying

This method of cooking is great for fillets or fish steaks. Melt a little butter or oil in a pan and allow the pan to heat up so the butter foams. Place in the fish. Make sure the fish browns on one side before you turn it, and then brown the other side. The fish should be cooked by now but use the skewer test on thick pieces of fish.

Roasting

This method is superb with larger portions of fish such as tuna or cod loin. Preheat the oven to 200°C/400°F/gas mark 6. Place fish portions of the same size (so it all cooks at the same rate) in a roasting tin; do not allow them to touch. Flavour with olive oil, garlic and perhaps some lemon and roast uncovered for between 8–15 minutes. Use the skewer test to check the fish is cooked before serving.

Grilling

Grilling is suitable for delicate pieces of fish that would break up if moved about too much, for example fillets of sole. Preheat the grill and place the fillets onto an oiled baking sheet (this could be sprinkled with herbs or crumbs). Cook without turning as the metal baking sheet conducts the heat to cook from beneath. Exact cooking times are difficult as fillets can be all sorts of different sizes. A more accurate way is to keep monitoring and cook until the flesh changes from translucent to opaque and the fish is extremely hot.

Deep or shallow frying

For this method the fish is coated in egg and breadcrumbs (or batter) to protect it from the fierce heat. Allow the oil to get really hot; test it by adding a crust of bread – if the oil is hot enough it should brown gently in about 15–20 seconds. Remove the bread and fry the fish in small batches. Drain on kitchen paper and sprinkle with salt to remove excess oil and to season. Remember fish cooks very quickly so keep a close eye on it.

cheese & eggs

If you've got eggs and cheese in the fridge then you'll always be able to rustle up something quick and tasty.

great for quick dishes

cheese

Cheese is always made from milk, although taste and texture will vary tremendously, depending on the milk used and how it's been made. Choosing types of cheese is down to personal taste and depends upon what you are selecting the cheese for: whether for a particular recipe or for the cheese board.

There are several ways to categorise cheese; here are some types and their uses:

- Fresh unripened cheese — Uncured and unripened, such as fromage blanc and fresh ricotta. These are not aged and must be used at once. They often have a sharp flavour and are wonderful served with fruit. These also include cream cheese for cheesecakes, good mozzarella for salads and the cheaper kinds for melting on pizzas.
- Soft cheeses — Brie, Camembert and Dolcelatte. Used for cheese boards, spreading on bread and in cooking.
- Semi hard — Edam, Gouda, Stilton and some Cheddars. Used for cheese boards and in cooking.
- Hard — Cheddar, Emmental, Gruyère. Used for cheese boards and in cooking.
- Very hard — Parmesan. Used for cooking and shavings to garnish.

storing cheese

Ideally cheese should be wrapped in paper or cheesecloth and stored in a cool cellar. For most of us this is just not possible so we store it in the fridge in a plastic bag or clingfilm. Unwrapped cheese will dry out and crack. Mass produced cheese will always be the same and somewhat characterless. A good cheese shop should only sell cheeses that are ready to eat, therefore at their peak.

The cheese board

One good cheese can be served at the end of a meal rather than lots of smaller pieces, but for a more varied choice go for one hard cheese, one soft cheese and perhaps a fresh cheese such as goats' cheese. Cheese should be served at cool room temperature, so allow it to have a few hours out of the fridge before serving.

Accompany with fruit such as grapes, figs, apples and celery, chutneys can also provide a tangy contrast to the cheese. Keep it simple and choose just one or two of the above to go with the cheese and don't forget the crackers.

Cooking with cheese

Some cheeses melt better than others, and it is this that determines which cheese to use in a particular recipe. Cheese becomes tough and stringy if overheated and this should be avoided. A good melting cheese is high in fat and not too dry.

Hot tip

Buy a lump of fresh Parmesan without too much rind. You can grate it when you need it or take off shavings with a potato peeler to garnish salads. It keeps well in a large piece,

wrapped up in clingfilm and kept in the fridge. At all costs, avoid packet Parmesan cheese, which smells and tastes like bad feet!

eggs

Eggs are so useful and versatile, from setting custards to lifting cakes and soufflés. Where would we be without them? They should be kept in the fridge, pointed end down, and away from strong smells, as they are porous and things such as onions can taint them.

I always buy free-range eggs and believe they taste better. Battery-farmed eggs will only be on sale as long as there is a demand for them.

Hot tip

To tell if eggs are fresh place an egg in a bowl of cold water. If it floats it is not fresh. This is because the egg has a small air sack in it, and the older the egg, the larger the air sack becomes. You may also spin the egg. If it spins on the spot it is fresh. Again this is due to the air sack becoming larger and sending the egg off centre.

Separating eggs

To separate the yolk from the white you should crack the egg on the edge of a bowl and then open it with the pointed end uppermost (do this over the bowl). The yolk will be in the bottom half and most of the white will drop into the bowl. Then carefully pour the yolk from half to half until all the white has gone. If you do break the yolk you can lift out any yolk bits from the white using the shell.

Cooking eggs

To fry an egg: heat a little butter in a pan until barely hot; break the egg into the pan and leave to cook gently. Really it should not be called frying as such fierce heat would make the egg tough. You may spoon hot butter over the yolk to cook it.

To poach an egg: bring a small pan of water to the boil. Add a tablespoon of vinegar (this helps to set the protein in the egg). Take an egg straight from the fridge and break it into a cup. Swirl the water in the pan with a slotted spoon. Drop the egg into the middle and

immediately turn the pan down to simmering. You may follow it with another egg as the first egg swirls round the pan. It really works! When the eggs are cooked, remove with the slotted spoon and allow to drain briefly on kitchen paper. Serve with hot buttered toast, Yum!

For a perfect omelette for one: break two eggs into a bowl and season with salt and pepper. Beat with a fork until well mixed. Heat a thumb-sized knob of butter in an omelette pan and allow it to foam. Tip in the egg mixture and let it cover the bottom of the pan. As it cooks draw the edges into the middle with a fork. Keep going with this until the eggs are almost set, but a little creamy in the centre. Remove the pan from the heat and tip the pan so that the omelette slides over to one side of the pan. Add your prepared filling to one side and using a fork fold the omelette in half. Have your plate ready and tip the omelette onto it.

Scrambled egg is similar to making an omelette but you stir the egg in the saucepan with a lot more vigour and do not let the bottom set. You may also add a little milk to the eggs. See page 14 for a microwave method.

To cook boiled eggs: place the eggs in a pan of cold water and bring to the boil, simmering for ten minutes for hard-boiled eggs and time four minutes in already boiling water for a soldier-dipping yolk. Alternatively, add your eggs to a pan of boiling water, turn down the heat and simmer for twelve minutes. Place the boiled eggs in cold water to cool rapidly before peeling.

store cupboard

When cooking meals every day and shopping perhaps only every few days or once a week, it pays to have a well-stocked store cupboard or larder. You may buy meat or vegetables with no real idea of what they will become. However, if the store cupboard has everything it should have, then making any recipe or idea from a book, the internet or your head can easily be achieved. You don't have to go out and buy all of these at once; just buy them as you need them and replace them when necessary, and soon you'll find your store cupboard is brimming with ideas.

the larder is the backbone of the kitchen!

Basics

Use ordinary olive oil and sunflower oil for cooking. Plain flour is useful for batters and gravy, as well as for cake making if you add raising agents such as baking soda. For thickening sauces, keep cornflour and arrowroot powder. Both should be mixed into a paste with a little cold water before adding to your sauce. Cornflour requires more cooking than arrowroot and produces an opaque finish, while arrowroot makes a clear sauce so is better for sweet sauces.

Baking

It doesn't take many ingredients to knock up a quick sponge cake or a few biscuits and if you keep a number of stock ingredients in supply you'll be able to make a number of sweet treats whenever you fancy.

Self-raising flour has the raising agent already in the flour and is great for making cakes. Baking powder, bicarbonate of soda, cream of tartar and cocoa powder are also useful for baking and making cakes.

A number of sugars and sweetening agents are useful, have a supply of the following and you'll be able to complete most recipes:

- icing sugar
- soft brown sugar
- demerara sugar
- caster sugar
- golden syrup
- clear honey

Baking and dessert recipes often call for vanilla, either vanilla essence or pods, you should stay clear of the nasty bottles labelled 'flavouring' which have a poor taste in comparison.

Buy some good quality cooking chocolate (look for cocoa solids of 70 per cent. This means it is really good quality and it usually has a one year sell-by date so it won't go off if you aren't planning an immediate chocolate fest). If you can't find decent cooking chocolate buy good-quality eating chocolate with a high cocoa solids percentage, don't buy bars of chocolate-flavoured cake covering which are best reserved for children's parties.

Nuts, such as pine nuts, hazelnuts, walnuts and almonds are all great for baking and can also be used to jazz up salads. You'll find nuts sold either whole, chopped, flaked or ground; stock up on what you use most frequently or, if you have a food processor, buy them whole and prepare them yourself as required.

Dressings, sauces, marinades and gravies

Don't overlook the ingredients needed to make your accompanying sauces, if you use poor-quality ingredients in the condiments then your perfectly-cooked dish could be ruined.

For simply dressings, sauces, marinades and gravies keep the following in stock:

- Mustards – these are a great way to inject flavour into a dressing or plain white sauce to serve with ham or a gammon steak. Mustards don't like to be boiled so add them at the end of the cooking and whisk in. Try wholegrain mustard, Dijon mustard or English mustard and appreciate the differences in each.
- Vinegar – red wine vinegar, white wine vinegar and balsamic vinegar are all good for salad dressings, as is extra virgin olive oil.
- Stock cubes – have a supply of beef, chicken, fish, lamb and vegetable cubes.
- Wine – decent red and white wine can be used for marinades, gravies and stews – as a guide you'll have a far tastier sauce if you use a wine you'd drink rather than a bottle of plonk.
- Table sauces – for stir fries and marinating keep a supply of soy sauce, Asian fish sauce (nam pla), oyster sauce, plum sauce, Worcestershire sauce, tabasco sauce, tomato purée and tomato sauce.
- For quick pasta dishes keep such things as tinned tomatoes, tapenade (black olive paste), olives, sun-dried tomatoes (dried or in oil), salted capers and tinned anchovies.
- Pesto is also a great store cupboard ingredient.

Carbs

For many a meal isn't complete without some form of carbohydrate – even though the woman in your life may be in the throws of some no-carb diet. Potatoes are arguably the most popular but there are plenty of dried options that should have a permanent home in your cupboard.

Dried pasta of all shapes and sizes are really useful, and rice, both arborio (a white rice used for risottos, see page 41) and basmati, is a brilliant store cupboard stand-by. For something a little more unusual try couscous – a great partner for fish or meat dishes. Pour on enough boiling stock or water to just cover the couscous and cover with a plate or clingfilm. After a few minutes stir through with a fork. Add fresh chopped herbs and lemon juice for a really delicious taste. See page 81 for a recipe idea.

Tinned pulses are a real winner as they can be used as the protein, the carbohydrate or the vegetable part of a meal. You can make a super cheat's cassoulet or a delicious tuna salad with tinned beans. Try borlotti beans, cannellini beans, butter beans, red kidney beans, chickpeas or haricot beans.

Similarly lentils, such as red, yellow or Puy, are useful as an alternative to potatoes. Cooked with stock and finished with herbs they are really exciting and should shake off their boring vegetarian image.

Cooking pasta & rice

To cook dried pasta: add the pasta to a large pan of boiling, salted water (with a teaspoon of salt). Use about 85 g/3 oz pasta per person for a normal main course portion. Stir once as the water comes back up to the boil and cook rapidly without a lid for the recommended time; different shapes of pasta will take different times. The pasta should be *al denté* – just cooked – and if you cut the pasta shape in half there should be no white starch visible. Drain and use straight away – don't let it sit, but add your sauce or dressing immediately.

Cooking rice seems to be one of those things that can cause panic and arguments all round. There are several ways of cooking and they are all as good as each other. The real thing is to use whichever method works best for you. The following method is straightforward and easy to follow, and if people tell you you are doing it wrong, just ignore them – this way is as good as any other.

Long grain, basmati, Thai rice, brown rice and wild rice can be cooked in the following way: allow 55 g/2 oz uncooked rice per person. Begin by washing the rice in cold water, using a sieve. Rinse until the water runs clear. Then place the rice into a large pan of boiling lightly salted water . Stir once as the water returns to the boil and turn down to a very low simmer so that the water is just moving gently. Leave uncovered. Cook for 8–10 minutes (brown rice will take a bit longer – always check the timings on the packet for different recommended cooking times) and test by eating a bit. It should feel tender and, like pasta, if you cut a grain in half it should have no white starch visible in the middle.

Once cooked, strain immediately into a colander or sieve. Leave to steam over the pan for a few minutes. You can fork through it gently to prevent the grains sticking together. Stir through any chopped fresh herbs, cooked peas or chopped peppers for colour.

For lemon-scented rice, cook as above and stir through the zest of two lemons and some fresh chopped coriander. To cook a speciality rice such as arborio, closely follow the guidelines on the packet.

Herbs and spices

Herb and spices often form the 'secret' ingredient in a successful dish and clever experimentation with them can lead to some great flavours. It may take time to develop a well-stocked collection but drop one item into the shopping trolley each week and you'll get there soon enough. Then you can let your imagination run wild.

The bare essential to your supplies should be salt and pepper. Rock sea salt and whole black peppercorns in particular are necessary for your salt and pepper mills.

Spices are useful for both sweet and savoury dishes. Try the following: ground all-spice, ground cinnamon, ground coriander, ground cumin, ground ginger, whole nutmeg, garam masala, cardamom pods, cayenne, chilli powder, chilli flakes, peppercorns, paprika and turmeric. All of the above are good choices but remember to buy spices in small quantities as they do lose their flavour if kept for too long.

Dried herbs are also good items, especially during the winter when fresh herbs are scarce. They are particularly good in stews. Start with oregano, basil, mixed herbs and thyme.

Dried herbs win on convenience but fresh herbs still have more flavour and although I'm not particularly green fingered, I do grow my own parsley, bay, oregano, rosemary, lemon and ordinary thyme. In the summer I grow basil and fresh chillies. Try fresh home-grown herbs and enjoy the satisfaction of not always paying supermarket prices. You can also keep a small quantity of fresh garlic and ginger in the fridge. If you enjoy Thai cooking only now and again then you can freeze kaffir lime leaves, galangal and lemon grass.

Hot tip

If you do grow your own herbs one way to enjoy them all year round to freeze small handfuls in ice cube trays. Put the freshly cut herbs into the compartments, cover with water and fast freeze. To use them just pop one or two cubes directly into your dish.

In the fridge

The fridge can also be stocked with the dietary staples such as butter, milk, eggs, sour cream, cheese and Greek yoghurt that can take the place of double cream. Obviously these cannot be purchased too far in advance, as they need to be used while still fresh.

Sundries

There are always other ingredients that will be needed, the ones listed here are not always needed but I like to keep of supply of them in my kitchen:

- Fresh white bread for making crumbs. The crumbs you buy in supermarkets always seem to be a horrid orange colour.
  - Keep a few citrus fruits in your fruit bowl – oranges, lemons and limes. Add them to a dressing or use them to flavour fish.
- Dried mushrooms are fantastic; they provide masses of flavour for stews, rice and pasta dishes and make great stock.

Now you should have all you need. Some of the ingredients that have been featured are particularly suited to certain methods of cooking, and that is how I have listed them. But don't be limited by this. If you have bought some nuts for baking and then want to use them to jazz up a salad, that's the first step to inventing your own recipes. Experiment and enjoy!

veggie store cupboard

Supermarkets and restaurants are now much more aware of vegetarians and the days of just a stuffed pepper or limp veggie lasagne are gone. Cooking for vegetarian guests needn't be a nightmare either as with a little thought you can create something to be proud of which you won't have to hide from the meat eaters.

it pays to be well-stocked

Basics about the vegetarian diet

All the nutrients you need can easily be obtained from a vegetarian diet. In fact research shows that in many ways a vegetarian diet is healthier than that of a typical meat eater. Vegetarians can obtain protein from the following:

- Nuts: hazels, brazils, almonds, cashews, walnuts, pine kernels, etc.
- Seeds: sesame, pumpkin, sunflower and linseeds.
- Pulses: peas, beans, lentils and peanuts.
- Grains/cereals: wheat (in bread, flour, pasta etc), barley, rye, oats, millet, maize (sweetcorn) and rice.
- Soya products: tofu, textured vegetable protein, veggieburgers and soya milk.
- Dairy products: milk, cheese, yoghurt and free-range eggs.

Meat substitutes explained

Many vegetarians do not use meat substitutes, but if you do want an alternative for the meat or fish in a recipe, you can use quorn or one of the many soya products available.

TVP, which stands for textured vegetable protein, was one of the first meat substitute products to emerge. Often called dried soya mince, it is a by-product of the soya oil industry, and is made from the remaining soya flour once the oil has been extracted. Very low in fat and a good source of fibre, it comes as dried chunks, mince or flakes, to which you add water before using it in a recipe. There's no flavour to it, but its sponge-like texture means it marinates and absorbs flavours well in cooking. It has a realistic meat-like texture, especially in traditional mince dishes such as lasagne and spaghetti bolognese.

Quorn products are healthy, delicious and meat-free. The unique ingredient in all quorn foods is mycoprotein which is a nutritious member of the fungus family – as are mushrooms, and truffles – and provides the taste and texture of a full range of meat products and ready meals. As well as the prepared ready meals, you can buy quorn pieces and mince, to use in your own cooking. Use the pieces in place of chicken and the mince for dishes that would usually use minced meat, such as cottage pie.

Tofu or soya bean curd is a soft, cheese-like food made by curdling soya milk with a coagulant, is it normally sold in one rectangular block which can then be cut into cubes and used in a similar way to quorn and TVP. It has the same ability to pick up flavours although it has little flavour of its own.

Nut roast is the classic vegetarian equivalent of a roast joint of meat, and these can vary in ingredients enormously, depending on the type of nut you like and which herbs you use. A handy cheat is to stock vegetarian stuffing mix, which you can bulk out with chopped mixed nuts, breadcrumbs and maybe an egg to bind. Feel free to chuck in sauces, herbs and spices of your choice.

It's all about experimenting, so enjoy yourself!

go organic

There are many reasons to shop organically; the only reason not to do so seems to be the price. The more people who demand organic meat, dairy produce, fruit and vegetables the more the price will drop.

Eating seasonally and as locally as possible has to be the way forward to cut down on food miles and helping to counteract environmental damage and global warming. You may decide to be selective about which foods you buy organic, whether for cost reasons or convenience. It is worth reading up about whether some foods are better than others to buy organic — for example it has been suggested that pulses and root vegetables, such as carrots, concentrate the chemicals and pesticides inside them, which can pose serious health risks to the consumer. Ultimately it has to be a matter of personal choice, but the more knowledge we have, the more able we are to make an informed decision.

Reasons for an organic kitchen

- Food safety — organic farmers, as far as possible, avoid using unnecessary chemical sprays. Food additives linked to asthma and heart disease are among those banned under organic standards.
- The environment — organic farming is friendlier to the environment so there is a much greater diversity of birds, butterflies and plants on organic farms. Organic standards ban the use of GM technology.
- Animal welfare — organic farming requires animals to be kept in more natural, free-range conditions with a more natural diet.
- Taste — many people buy organic because they say it tastes better.
- Traceability — it is all about knowing where the food we eat comes from. We don't need to know what the animal had for breakfast, lunch and dinner but that it has had as natural a life as possible.
- Local support — organic food is often sourced locally. So by eating organically you'll be supporting local farmers and producers too.

health & safety

To avoid food poisoning it's important to make sure the food you make for yourself and others is safe to eat. There are a few basic rules to help you make sure of this.

good food is safe food

Buying

Only buy fresh food from sources that you trust.

Washing

Wash all food if it is to be eaten raw, even if the food is to be peeled such as carrots and potatoes.

Your fridge

This should stay roughly at 4°C. It is important not to overfill it as this cuts down on circulation of the cool air. Refrigerate all meat, fish, chicken, dairy products and eggs. Keep dairy products at the top of the fridge and always cover raw meat and store it on the bottom shelf of the fridge where it can't touch or drip onto other foods. Try to rotate the food in your fridge and cupboards, so the oldest stuff is eaten first. Never put warm or hot food in the fridge as this will warm up the temperature inside. Wait until it reaches room temperature before refrigerating.

Raw meat

Raw meat contains harmful bacteria that can spread very easily to anything it touches, including other foods, worktops, chopping boards, hands and knives. It's especially important to keep raw meat away from ready-to-eat foods, such as salad, fruit and bread. This is because these foods won't be cooked before you eat them, so bacteria that gets onto these foods won't be killed. To help stop bacteria from spreading, remember these things:

- Don't let raw meat touch other foods.
- Never prepare ready-to-eat food using a chopping board or knife

that you have used to prepare raw meat,
unless they have been washed thoroughly first.

- Always wash hands, knives, boards and anything else
  in contact with raw meat or fish, with cold water
  first to wash off the meat juices, then with hot
  soapy water and scrub well. Allow items to air dry
  before putting away and ensure that boards stand
  upright with air able to circulate round them.
- Change cloths and tea towels at least once a day
- Use an anti-bacterial spray on kitchen surfaces
  before and after each cooking session.

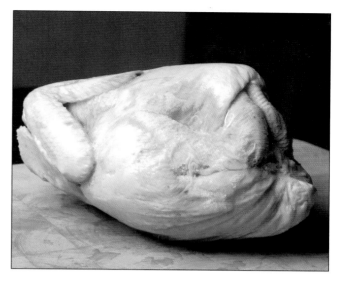

Cooking

Always make sure you preheat the oven before placing food
inside. Cook food thoroughly to kill any bacteria that may be
present. Remember that pregnant women cannot eat raw or
unpasturised eggs, watch out in particular for mayonnaise
dishes and make sure all eggs are thoroughly cooked. The old
and very young may have lower immune systems and
therefore also need well-cooked eggs.

Reheating food.

If you need to reheat food, make sure it is very hot through
to the centre, and when keeping food warm make sure it is
thoroughly hot first then maintain a good holding
temperature that will keep it really hot, not just lukewarm.

Freezing & thawing

When freezing food, label and clearly mark with the date.
Never refreeze thawed food without cooking it first. Thaw
food overnight in the fridge, on a plate or in a plastic
container in case of drips. Allow enough time for
food to completely thaw; in the case of a
Christmas turkey this could take a couple of days.

Cooling

When cooling food for storage, try to cool as
fast as possible, so bacteria doesn't have time to
grow. Never cover with a lid while cooling, as this
slows things down. Never cover with clingfilm
either as this acts just like a lid and provides
warm, humid conditions perfect for bacteria.
I always tip food out onto a plate or tray to
cool rapidly. Never leave food out overnight to
cool; try to get it in the fridge within an hour
of cooking.

If any thing smells or looks bad, don't eat it. Food
which actually looks 'off' is probably well on its
way to deteriorating.

food presentation

People eat with their eyes first and if food looks fresh and inviting you are off to a good start. Always make time to present the food on nice plates or in larger dishes; there is nothing worse than that 'chuck it on the plate' version of presentation.

good presentation will give your food a head start

Serving at the table can be rather fraught, and there is also the risk of the food getting cold by the time everyone is served. So it is often preferable to present individual servings, which can be arranged in the kitchen and brought straight to the table. This kind of service must be done on hot plates or your food will quickly go cold.

Whether it is rustic and homely food or if you are having a stab at more up market presentation the rules are the same. Here are some simple guidelines to ensure well-presented, stylish and delicious-looking food.

- Keep it hot; always serve food on hot plates. Don't plan complicated presentations so that the food gets cold.

- Keep it simple and fresh looking, remember, less is more, when playing with food. Don't try to be too clever, keep the presentation clean and uncluttered.

- The right crockery is important if you want to impress with your presentation. Large white plates are in vogue at present and allow the food to speak for itself. The space also allows the cook to create more interest in the food. Whatever you choose, however, ensure that the plates are in keeping with the food. Use rustic bowls to serve spaghetti and other homely types of food and elegant white china for more stylish cuisine.

- Keep the garnish relevant and edible. For example; a sprig of fresh watercress complements lamb nicely. The texture, taste and colour all do something for the lamb and you can happily eat it; in contrast a bunch of rosemary, even though it might provide the colour and relevant fragrance, is unpleasant to eat. When adding garnish to salads or trifles, placing olives or cherries in a pattern may sound like a good idea but it can look childish. In general avoid symmetry when arranging food and remember odd numbers work better than even, especially smaller numbers.

- Centre height: when serving any food that can be nicely piled up; such as meringues or profiteroles, or even pieces of meat in a casserole, try to arrange them with centre height rather than flat across the plate. This makes it look interesting and draws the eye to the food – it also helps keep things warm. When garnishing food with centre height, place the garnish to one side rather than in the middle or on the top.

- The right amount: ensure the plates of food look like a generous portion. If you don't have enough of something it just looks stingy to use a tiny bit. On the other hand don't fill the plate to capacity just because you want to use something up.

- As a handy guide for when you're eating out, or even if you want to impress at home, I've included a diagram of a formal table setting so you know exactly what to use and for what. As a general rule though use the outer cutlery first and work in towards the plate.

1.	Napkin	9.	Soup spoon
2.	Fish/starter fork	10.	Bread plate
3.	Dinner fork	11.	Butter knife
4.	Salad fork	12.	Dessert spoon
5.	Service plate		& fork
6.	Soup bowl	13.	Water glass
7.	Dinner knife	14.	White wine glass
8.	Fish/starter knife	15.	Red wine glass

wine

this is a matter of taste & bank balance

The subject of wine is exhaustive and this book is not the place to start an in-depth study. Essentially you need to know what goes with what and more importantly what you like to drink. Some food is perfect with an expensive red or a classic dry white, but this is a matter of taste and bank balance. What you spend on wine is up to you, but there are many good value wines available both to accompany food or to drink on their own. Ultimately choose what you like to drink. If you prefer red wine with your desserts or white wine with roast beef, that's up to you.

For those that want more general assistance, I suggest you match sweet wine with sweet food, acidic wine with acidic or salty food, spicy wine with spicy food, red wine with red meat and white wine with white meat and fish. As we are not a great wine-producing nation ourselves, we seem to embrace wine from all over the world without snobbery. The best advice is to try a new wine each time you cook a new dish and take suggestions or recommendations from specialist wine shops. Each of my recipes features a suggested wine or drink to accompany the dish, feel free to substitute with other drinks and as a further source of reference here is a general guide to matching wine with food.

- Muscadet or other light dry whites for shellfish and moules marinière.

- Reds such as Bordeaux, Burgundy, Pinot Noir, Chateauneuf du Pape, Malbec or Cabernet-Sauvignon for roast beef or a beef casserole.

- Heavy reds such as Australian Shiraz and Barolo go well with rich stews, venison and other game.

- Unoaked Chardonnay from Australia, Chablis, Chenin Blanc or Sauvignon Blanc go well with white meats.

- For lamb dishes, try medium reds such Claret, Côte du Rhone, Pinot Noir, Zinfandel from Chile, Merlots from Australia, Bulgaria, Hungary, New Zealand, South Africa and the USA.

- If you are barbecuing, chilled rosé or fruity Beaujolais are great, particularly with chargrilled salmon or tuna.

- You need stronger wines to stand up to marinated or spicy food: try a full-bodied California Zinfandel, Merlot (or Cabernet Sauvignon/Merlot blend), Spanish Rioja or Côtes du Rhone. Expensive wines are a waste when it comes to really spicy food; try German or Australian Riesling and Chenin Blanc.

- For curry stick with beer or chance a rosé as it won't overpower the food too much.

- For pasta match the wine with the sauce and try a Sauvignon Blanc for a tomato-based sauce, while a full-bodied Merlot will complement the richer meaty flavour of a lasagne or Bolognese. Cream or butter pasta sauces need the lighter touch of either a Chardonnay or Semillon.

- Wines with citrus and freshness go well with oily fish; Italian Chardonnay or gooseberry-flavoured Sauvignon Blanc from New Zealand are good bets.

- With white fish, look again at the accompanying sauce, following the same rule as for pasta. No wine should overpower the food.

- If you are serving smoked fish you need a little more power. Try white French Burgundy, Riesling or Californian Chardonnay. Rosé wines are also very good with smoked fish.

- Salads are served with vinegar-based dressings and these are a killer to many wines, making them taste like vinegar. Choose an acidic wine to complement them, such as Sauvignon

Blanc. Riesling makes a good choice for many salads, as it is not so assertive that it will overpower the salad's flavours.

- Wine and cheese are delicious together; the French always have cheese before dessert so that the red wine, had with the main course, can be finished. Mature Cheddar is perfectly suited to something fruity like a New Zealand Pinot Noir or a juicy Syrah. Also try Australian Cabernet Sauvignon or Chilean Zinfandel. Many cheeses will overpower good red wine – Roquefort is a good example, so choose your cheese carefully.

- Sweet wines are not always served, but for a special occasion try an orange Muscat or a sweet sherry. Serve Champagne or Asti Spumante with rich creamy puddings and try a honeyed Sauternes with strawberries and cream.

using the recipes

As well as a drink suggestion, each recipe has a difficulty indicator. This is a rating out of five, one being easiest. Here's a breakdown of what to expect from each rating:

1. Dead easy, in fact you may already have made a recipe like this before.

2. Moments of confusion, but you'll soon get into the swing of things.

3. A few complicated bits, but it's likely to just be issues of timing rather than anything too fiddly.

4. Your skills might be stretched by dishes at this level but keep your cool and you'll be fine.

5. Tackle these dishes when you're more confident, the results will always be worth the effort but it's wise to give yourself plenty of time when cooking these recipes. They tend to use several skills and techniques.

Don't shy away from the more difficult dishes, if you never attempt the harder ones you'll never improve. Get friends round and experiment on them if you don't want to force your efforts onto your partner or guests just yet.

The other information you'll find for each recipe includes preparation and cooking times. Don't be put off by these either. Often a long preparation time will mean you can prepare it in advance and cook later, similarly a long cooking time generally means you'll be able to leave it in the oven and get on with something else. Always read the recipe through before you begin, then you'll know exactly where the tricky parts are and you'll be far less likely to miss out vital ingredients.

Most of the recipes serve four people but you can easily divide or multiply the quantities to correspond with your number of guests.

Lastly, at the top of the information boxes you'll notice little symbols. These indicate the primary ingredient(s) for that recipe, I've divided all the recipes into groups of:

- Meat (pages 54–87)

- Fish (pages 88–97)

- Vegetarian, including pasta & rice (pages 98–104)

- Eggs and cheese (pages 106–113)

 • Potato and vegetables (pages 114–119)

 • Puddings (pages 120–133)

After the recipes I've included a section with suggested menus (page 134–136) so you can put the dishes together to form a feast fit for any occasion.

home-made burger

Fantastic to barbecue and so easy to make. They freeze well and are so much better than ones you buy.

Preparation time: 15 minutes

Cooking time: 8 minutes

Serves: 4–6

Level of difficulty: 1

Drink suggestion: robust red/beer

1. Place all the ingredients into a large bowl, and, with a clean hand, mix until completely combined.

2. Drape a piece of clingfilm over a plate. Divide the mince into six lots then place a large pastry cutter* on a plate on top of the clingfilm. Press the mixture down into the cutter and smooth flat with your fingers or a spoon.

3. Remove the cutter then use the clingfilm to move the burger to another plate.

4. Repeat with the remaining mixture and chill the burgers until you are ready to cook.

5. Thoroughly preheat the grill or barbecue, cook each side for 3–5 minutes until cooked to your preference. When you first put them onto the barbecue don't try to move them for at least two minutes, they will easily be turned with a fish slice after that time if the barbecue is hot enough.

Ingredients

675 g/1½ lb lean best steak mince

1 medium onion, peeled and grated

3 tbsp finely chopped parsley and chives

1 tbsp Worcestershire sauce

salt and freshly ground black pepper

a pinch of cayenne pepper (optional)

or, a dash of tomato sauce (optional

Note

* I use a large pastry cutter to shape the burgers and they never fall apart. If you don't have a cutter just shape them by hand or use a plastic tub (the sort that comes with hummus or taramasalata). Simply press the mix into the tub firmly, then tap the container onto the tray to produce your burger. The burgers can be frozen once shaped. Just defrost overnight in the fridge on a plate or tray.

beef cooked in stout with dumplings

A deliciously warming and comforting dish perfect for a chilly winter's day. This dish can be frozen without the dumplings, so double the quantities and have a handy and wholesome meal ready for reheating.

Preparation time: 30 minutes
Cooking time: 2 hours
Serves: 4
Level of difficulty: 2
Drink suggestion: beer or robust red wine

Ingredients

675 g/1 ½ lb chuck or stewing steak

1 tbsp oil

2 onions, finely sliced

1 tsp soft brown sugar

1 garlic clove, crushed

2 tsp plain flour

440 ml (1 can) stout

300 ml/ ½ pint beef stock

1 bay leaf

a pinch of thyme

salt and freshly ground black pepper

1. When buying your beef try to buy it in large pieces, trimming off any hard fat. Leave the meat in large steaks, it's easier to brown. Heat half the oil in a large heavy frying pan and allow it to get very hot. Add the beef and brown on both sides.

2. Place the meat and any juices into a large oven-proof casserole dish.

3. Preheat the oven to 150°C/300°F/gas mark 2.

4. Check the frying pan is not burnt* and add the rest of the oil and the onions and cook over a much lower temperature until beginning to soften (about five minutes).

(continued overleaf)

Note
* If the pan is burnt you can usually smell it, if you are not sure: add a little water and bring to the boil then taste the mixture. If it tastes burnt chuck it out and rinse out the pan with fresh water. Then continue with the recipe.

5. Add the sugar and turn up the heat to brown the onions, scraping the bottom of the pan. Add the garlic and the flour and stir in, coating the onions. Once the ingredients are brown but not burnt add the stout and the stock.

6. Bring to the boil and stir to release all the flavour from the bottom of the pan. Pour the sauce over the meat in the casserole dish and bring slowly to the boil.

7. Ensure the meat is covered in liquid (just top up with water if you need to). Add the bay leaf, thyme, salt and freshly ground black pepper.

8. Put the lid on the dish and cook in the oven for at least two hours. After the cooking time is up check to see if the meat is absolutely tender; it should break with a spoon. If there is too much liquid you may remove the meat and boil the sauce on the stove top to reduce it. Stir it now and again to prevent it catching. When you are happy with the consistency (it should be shiny, syrupy and rich in taste) return the meat to the pan, check the seasoning and don't forget to remove the bay leaf. The dumplings (see next section) may be served on top, all in the one pot and make sure you clean the outside surface of the pot if you intend to serve it at the table.

dumplings

Preparation time: 10 minutes

Cooking time: 30 minutes

Serves: 4 (makes 8 dumplings)

Level of difficulty: 1

Ingredients

225 g/8 oz self-raising flour

a pinch of salt

110 g/4 oz beef suet

12 tbsp cold water

570 ml/1 pint beef stock

1. Make the dumplings in the last half hour of the cooking time of the casserole. Sift the flour and salt into a bowl and mix in the suet.

2. Make a small well in the centre and add the cold water to form a soft, but not too sticky dough. With floured hands, form the dough into golf ball-sized balls.

3. Place the balls into the simmering stock and cook for about half an hour or until light and with no raw dough in the centre. They can be placed into the finished stew or served onto each guest's plate.

beef chilli

Without the chilli and kidney beans this recipe can be used as a meat sauce base for bolognese, lasagne and cottage pie. Serve it with rice, tortillas, tacos, as a pancake filling or with jacket potatoes.

Preparation time: 30 minutes

Cooking time: up to 2 hours in the oven

Serves: 4

Level of difficulty: 1

Drink suggestion: light red wine

Ingredients

450 g/1 lb lean minced beef

1 large onion, finely chopped

1 stick of celery, finely chopped

2 garlic cloves, crushed

1/2 teaspoon chilli flakes (or more, if you like it hotter)

800 g/1 lb 12 oz/2 tins chopped tomatoes

300 ml/ 1/2 pint beef stock (1 beef stock cube and water)

400 g/14 oz/ 1 tin red kidney beans, drained

salt and freshly ground black pepper

1. Heat a large heavy frying pan until quite hot but not smoking – you shouldn't need oil as there should be enough fat in the meat. Add the minced beef and spread it out over the base of the pan, don't overcrowd the pan do two lots if necessary. Allow it to brown well, turning frequently and breaking it up as it browns. Tip the mince into a sieve while you cook the sauce.

2. Lower the heat and add a tablespoon of fat to the pan (you can use the fat draining off the mince for this). Add the onion and celery, cover and gently sweat the ingredients. When the onions and celery begin to soften, add the garlic and dried chillies and cook for a few more minutes.

3. Add the tomatoes, stock and browned mince and bring to the boil. Add the kidney beans and turn the heat down very low to simmer for 1–1½ hours, stirring now and again to prevent it catching or see the hot tip below for oven cooking.

4. At the end of reducing the sauce, it should be slightly syrupy and the meat tender. Season with salt and freshly ground black pepper and accompany with rice (see page 41).

Hot tip

Once you have added the kidney beans you can transfer the chilli to an ovenproof casserole dish with a lid and cook in the oven for two hours on 150°C/300°F/gas mark 2. Long, slow cooking will give you a really tender and rich finish. Once the meat is tender you can simmer in the oven without a lid to evaporate some of the liquid to concentrate the flavour.

hot steak sandwich with rocket & horseradish

This sandwich is practically guaranteed to hit the spot every time and it hardly takes any time at all to prepare. Substitute the ciabatta with French stick or doorstop slices of crusty bread if you prefer.

Preparation time: 10 minutes

Cooking time: 10 minutes

Serves: 4

Level of difficulty: 1

Drink suggestion: light red wine

Ingredients

4 thin sirloin steaks

salt and freshly ground black pepper

1 tsp sunflower oil

2 small ciabatta loaves

15 g/ ½ oz unsalted butter

creamed horseradish and/or dijon mustard
to taste

2 handfuls of fresh rocket/watercress/mustard
leaves, washed

1. Season the steaks with salt and freshly ground black pepper.

2. Heat a frying pan or griddle and add the oil. Allow it to almost smoke and add the steak, cook to your preference (see page 27). Do this in two lots if the pan is small.

3. While the steak is cooking, slice both loaves horizontally and spread with the butter, followed by as much creamed horseradish or Dijon mustard, as you like.

4. Place the salad onto the bread. Once the steak is cooked place it on top of the salad and put the lid on the sandwiches. Slice each loaf into two and serve at once.

roast chicken with all the trimmings

A roast dinner never fails to impress and it really isn't that hard to master.

Preparation time: 15–30 minutes	
Cooking time: 2 hours	
Serves: 4	
Level of difficulty: 3	
Drink suggestion: almost any wine	

For the stuffing

2 tbsp sunflower oil

1 red onion, finely chopped

1 celery stick, finely chopped

4 garlic cloves, crushed

1 tsp thyme and rosemary, chopped

225 g/8 oz pork sausage meat

1 apple, grated with skin

85 g/3 oz fresh white breadcrumbs (place bread into a food processor to make crumbs)

salt and freshly ground black pepper

For the chicken and chipolatas

1.35 kg/3 lb free range chicken without giblets

1/2 an apple

sprigs of thyme and rosemary

salt and freshly ground black pepper

8 chipolata sausages

8 rashers of streaky bacon

For the gravy

1/2 litre/ 1pt water

2 tsp plain flour

1 chicken stock cube

For the potatoes and vegetables

8 medium-sized potatoes (maris piper, King Edward or desirée)

sunflower oil or dripping, this could be the fat leftover from a previous roast or you can buy it as a solid block in the refrigerated section of your supermarket.

450 g/1 lb vegetables. Choose two or three vegetables of your choice for example, mange tout, sugar snap peas, broccoli, courgettes or carrots. Use around 110 g/4 oz veg per person (see pages 22–24 for cooking times and methods) or use the recipe for quick roasted vegetables (see page 118).

To make the stuffing

1. Heat the oil in a small saucepan and add the onion, celery and garlic. Cook with a lid for ten minutes on a low heat until soft. Remove and place onto a plate to cool.

2. When the onion is cold, mix together all the remaining ingredients for the stuffing and season well. You can fry a bit in a pan with a little oil to check the seasoning.

Preparing the chicken

1. Using your finger, lift the skin at the neck end and slowly release the skin from the breast. Work at it and you should create enough space for most of the stuffing. Once the skin is released all over the breast, push the stuffing up and over the flesh. You want about 1 cm/ ½ in. of stuffing over the whole area. Once you start you can move your hand over the outside of the skin to evenly distribute the stuffing. The remaining stuffing (or all of it, if you don't fancy stuffing the breast) can be formed into golf ball-sized balls.

2. Place the apple and herbs inside the cavity of the bird. Season with salt and freshly ground black pepper. Place into a roasting tin, cover loosely with foil and put in the fridge until you want to cook it.

3. To prepare the bacon, use the side of a knife to stretch out the rashers. Cut in half widthways and roll each half into a tight roll, pinning them together with a cocktail stick. Place the bacon rolls into a small roasting tin with the chipolatas and stuffing balls. These can also be prepared in advance.

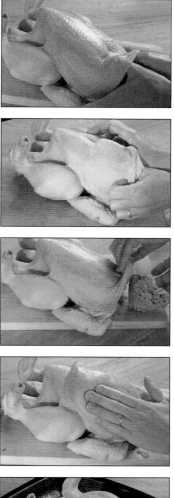

To cook the chicken

1. Preheat the oven to 200°C/400°F/gas mark 6. The chicken will need an hour and a half in the oven. (See page 29 for other cooking times if your bird is smaller or larger.) Place the chicken in the middle of the oven. After 30 minutes remove the foil.

2. After one hour place the chipolatas, bacon rolls and stuffing balls on the top shelf to cook.

3. After an hour and 15 minutes, test the chicken. Cut down between the breast and the leg. Let the leg fall open and use a knife to cut down to the thighbone. There should be no blood or pinkness.

4. If it is not yet cooked, return to the oven in another roasting tin, the other is needed to make the gravy. If it is cooked, remove the chicken and place onto a plate or a clean tin. Cover with foil and allow to rest while you make the gravy. It will stay hot.

To carve

Use a knife to remove the legs and cut in half at the joint. Using a sharp carving knife, cut slices from the breasts. The stuffing may become dislodged, but you can serve this alongside the chicken. Carve onto a large platter and cover with foil until you are ready to serve. Each person should get one piece of leg or thigh and some breast and stuffing. Alternatively, once you have removed the legs you can use kitchen scissors to completely remove the two breasts from the carcass. Then cut each breast in half again. You should have four pieces of leg and four pieces of breast which can then be served between your guests.

To make real gravy

1. Add half of the water to the roasting tin, scrape up the sediment with a wooden spoon and then pour all the juices from the tin into a small glass bowl, retain the roasting tin. Spoon off as much of the fat from the top of the juices as is possible, placing one tablespoon back in the roasting tin. The rest of the fat can be discarded but keep the juices which will be used later.

2. Place the tin on the hob over a very low heat and allow it to spit a bit; this is the water content evaporating leaving only fat.

3. Add two teaspoons of plain flour to the fat and stir well with a wooden spoon. Continue to stir and scrape, allow the mixture to brown gently, but don't allow it to smoke.

4. Once it is a good biscuit brown add the chicken juices from your glass bowl, the rest of the water and the stock cube. Turn up the heat and allow it to boil and reduce down to a thin, syrupy consistency, adding any extra juices from the resting chicken. This will take a good five minutes giving you time to carve the chicken. If you feel you need to you can sieve the gravy. Add more water if it looks too thick.

To make roast potatoes

1. Preheat the oven to 200°C/400°F/gas mark 6.

2. Use old potatoes, such as maris piper, King Edward or desirée, for best results. Wash, peel and cut them into large even-sized pieces. Place into a pan of cold salted water and bring to the boil with the lid on. Keeping the pieces large prevents them from absorbing too much water. You will cut them into roasting potato sizes later on.

3. Turn down to simmer for 5–10 minutes until barely tender. They should not be fully cooked. This is called par boiling. Place five tablespoons of sunflower oil or dripping into a roasting tin and place in the oven while it heats up.

4. Drain the potatoes (you can reserve the water for making the gravy) and allow to steam for five minutes. Return to the pan and shake to roughen the edges. This will give a crispier finish.

5. Check the fat in the oven. Once it's really hot, add the potatoes and cut each in half with a cutlery knife. This roughens the edges further. Shake the roasting tin gently and turn the potatoes with a fish slice to coat them in the oil.

6. Place into the oven for 45 minutes to an hour, turning twice with the fish slice during cooking. When done they will have a rough crusty edge and be deep golden brown. Season with salt and pepper before serving.

Timings for roast dinner

This assumes you have prepared the chicken and all your vegetables beforehand, which should only take 15–30 minutes.

11:00 Preheat the oven.

11:15 Chicken in the oven.

11:40 Par-boil the potatoes. Heat the oil for the roast potatoes.

12:00 Drain and roast potatoes. Move the chicken down to the bottom shelf of the oven to make room for the roast potatoes. Turn the potatoes at least twice during their cooking time.

12:15 Put the bacon rolls, chipolatas and stuffing balls in the oven. You can put them around the chicken if you are short of oven space.

12:40 Check the chicken – if it is not cooked return it to the oven in a different roasting tin while you make the gravy.

12:45 Gravy making and cooking of other vegetables (depending on cooking time of chosen vegetables). If your potatoes and trimmings are nice and brown turn the oven off but keep the door closed to keep everything hot.

12.50 Carve the chicken.

12:55 Remove all the trimmings from the oven and serve.

1.00 Dining.

Hot tip

The wonderful thing about a chicken roast dinner is that the chicken will hold without spoiling for a least half an hour, allowing you to catch up if you fall behind.

warm chicken salad

Serve this chicken salad as a lunch or a light supper — it's perfect for a summer's day when stoking up the barbecue seems too much effort.

Preparation time: 20 minutes

Cooking time: 15 minutes

Serves: 4

Level of difficulty: 1

Drink suggestion: light red wine

Ingredients

4 chicken breasts, trimmed of fat and skin

2 tbsp plain flour

salt and freshly ground black pepper

2 tbsp of sunflower oil

For the salad

4 handfuls of mixed small salad leaves such as rocket, watercress, lollo rosso, little gem; a prepared mixed bag is a good option

3 tbsp olive oil

1½ tbsp balsamic vinegar

salt and freshly ground black pepper

12 cherry tomatoes

½ cucumber, cut into large cubes

1. Cut the chicken breast into large pieces, about eight pieces from each breast.

2. Mix together the flour, salt and freshly ground black pepper. Roll the chicken in the flour mix and remove to a plate. Put the chicken pieces into a sieve to remove any excess flour.

3. Heat the oil in a large, heavy frying pan until hot but not smoking. Roll the chicken once again in the flour and shake off the excess using the sieve.

4. Fry the chicken in batches about twelve pieces at a time. Cook the chicken until it is golden brown and firm to the touch. It should take about four minutes. You may need to add a little more oil for the second batch. Place the chicken on kitchen paper once cooked while you assemble the salad.

5. Wash and dry the salad and mix the dressing by whisking the olive oil and balsamic vinegar together. Season with salt and freshly ground black pepper.

6. Place the salad in a large bowl with the cherry tomatoes, cucumber and dressing. Mix carefully and serve onto four plates. Put the chicken pieces on top of the salad and serve at once.

chicken breasts with shitake noodles

Until now you may have always stuck with bottled stir-fry sauces or opted for a takeaway but this dish will win your taste buds over. The chicken is also great on its own, try cooking it on the barbecue.

Preparation time: 30 minutes	
Cooking time: 20 minutes	
Serves: 4	
Level of difficulty: 2	
Drink suggestion: light red wine	

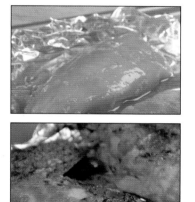

Ingredients for the marinade

4 chicken breasts, skinned

2 tbsp runny honey

2 tbsp light soy sauce

4 tsp grated fresh ginger

2 tbsp dry sherry

salt and freshly ground black pepper

(Ingredients continued on page 74)

1. Put the breasts into a plastic bag or bowl. Cover with the runny honey, light soy sauce, ginger, sherry and season. Leave to marinate for at least 30 minutes, up to 24 hours.

2. Preheat the grill.

3. Heat half of the groundnut oil in a wok and quickly stir fry the sliced peppers, mushrooms, red onion and spring onion (see page 74 for continued ingredients) for five minutes. Remove to a plate.

4. Place the marinated chicken into a roasting tin lined with foil. Put under the grill and cook for six minutes on each side or until the chicken is firm and hot all the way through. Baste the chicken with the marinade as you cook; it should be lightly caramelised because of the honey.

Ingredients for the noodles

2 tbsp groundnut oil

½ yellow, red and green pepper, deseeded and sliced

110 g/4 oz shitake mushrooms, sliced

1 red onion, sliced

2 spring onions, sliced

250 g/9 oz medium egg noodles

½ red and green chilli, deseeded and finely chopped

2.5 cm/1 inch grated fresh ginger, peeled and grated

1 large garlic clove, crushed

2.5 cm/1 inch finely chopped lemon grass

2 tbsp light soy sauce

2 tbsp mirin (see glossary on page 138)

1 tsp honey

salt and freshly ground black pepper

a handful of fresh coriander, roughly chopped

5. While the chicken is cooking, put the noodles in boiling water and cook for four minutes, or follow the instructions on the packet.

6. Heat the rest of the groundnut oil in the wok and fry the red chilli, green chilli, fresh ginger, garlic and lemon grass for one minute. Pour in the soy sauce, mirin and honey and cook for two minutes.

7. Return the vegetables to the wok and cook for one minute. Add the drained noodles to the wok; stir briefly, taste and season with salt and freshly ground black pepper.

8. Pile the vegetables and noodles onto four plates and serve the chicken on top. Sprinkle some fresh coriander over the dish to finish it off.

toad in the hole

For a more fancy toad you can serve individual ones cooked in little, flat ovenproof dishes. Have two sausages per dish and cook for about 15–20 minutes. They can be served in their dish as well. The batter recipe can also be used to make Yorkshire puddings for a roast dinner.

Preparation time: 40 minutes

Cooking time: 45 minutes

Serves: 4

Level of difficulty: 1

Drink suggestion: Côtes-du-Rhone

Ingredients

110 g/4 oz plain flour

a good pinch of salt

freshly ground black pepper

3 large eggs, beaten

300 ml/ ½ pint full fat milk and water mixed, or

300 ml/ ½ pint semi-skimmed milk

8 large good-quality sausages

4 tbsp beef dripping, vegetable or sunflower oil

1. Sift the flour, salt and pepper into a large bowl. Make a hole in the centre.

2. Put the beaten eggs into the hole and, working in a small circular motion, begin to incorporate the flour. When half the flour is mixed in, begin to add a little of the milk and water.

3. All of the flour should be mixed in by the time half the milk is added. Beat the batter to make it smooth and lump free then add the remaining liquid.

4. Sieve the batter if it contains lumps and chill for 20–30 minutes.

5. Meanwhile, brown the sausages by frying them in a pan with a little of the oil or dripping. Preheat the oven to 220°C/425°F/gas mark 7.

6. Heat the remaining dripping or oil in a shallow but large roasting tin, either in the oven while it preheats or over a direct heat. When almost smoking, place the sausages in at intervals and pour over the batter. Place in the top part of the oven and cook for at least 40 minutes or until the batter is risen, brown and crisp. Do not open the oven for the first 20–25 minutes as the batter will not rise properly. Glass-fronted ovens are great if you want to be able to peek at your food. Cut and serve with vegetables such as broccoli or green beans and onion gravy. If you like your toad with mash then see page 94.

onion gravy

Preparation time: 5 minutes

Cooking time: 15 minutes

Level of difficulty: 1

Ingredients

1 tbsp sunflower oil

1 medium onion, finely sliced

1 tsp plain flour

2 tbsp red wine/madeira/port

400 g/14 oz tinned French onion soup or beef consommé

salt and pepper

1. Heat the oil in a small pan and add the sliced onion. Cook gently for ten minutes with the lid on to soften.

2. Turn up the heat and brown the onion. When brown, add the flour, stir in and continue to cook.

3. When both onion and flour are brown add the red wine, madeira or port. Gently stir in.

4. Add the French onion soup or beef consommé. Bring to the boil and cook for about five minutes or until thickened and slightly syrupy.

5. Taste and season with salt and pepper. Serve over your toad in the hole.

spicy sausage & chickpea soup

This is a real man's soup, good and chunky with a spicy kick to it.

Preparation time: 15 minutes	
Cooking time: 45 minutes	
Serves: 4	
Level of difficulty: 1	
Drink suggestion: Italian or Spanish red wine	

Ingredients

1 large pinch saffron strands (optional)

2 tbsp olive oil

225 g/8 oz mini chorizo sausage or similar, cut into small cubes

½ tsp dried chilli flakes

2 garlic cloves, peeled and finely chopped

400 g/14 oz tinned chopped tomatoes

a pinch of sugar

400 g/14 oz tinned chickpeas, drained

285 g/10 oz new potatoes, quartered lengthways

1 bay leaf

1 litre/1¾ pints vegetable stock

salt and pepper

4 tbsp flat leaf parsley, freshly chopped (save a few leaves to garnish)

chilli oil (to serve)

1. Soak the saffron (if using) in a little warm water, set aside for ten minutes. Meanwhile, heat the oil in a large pan, add the sausage and cook for 2–3 minutes until golden brown. Drain and set aside.

2. Add the chilli flakes and garlic to the pan. Cook for 1–2 minutes. Stir in the tomatoes, sugar, chickpeas, potatoes, bay leaf, stock, saffron with its liquid and the sausage.

3. Bring to the boil, reduce the heat and simmer for 30 minutes with a lid on, stirring occasionally until the potatoes are cooked through and the mixture thickens slightly. Season with salt and pepper

4. Stir in most of the fresh parsley and spoon into individual soup bowls. Drizzle with a little chilli oil, sprinkle with the remaining parsley and serve with plenty of crusty bread.

Hot tip

By cooking this without a lid you can reduce the cooking liquid and make it into a thick stew instead of a soup.

lamb cutlets with spicy couscous

If you always struggle with cooking rice give couscous a try. A north African staple, couscous doesn't really need much cooking and is ready in five minutes. With quick cooked lamb cutlets this dish is real fast food.

Ingredients

225 g/8 oz couscous

300 ml/ ¹/₂ pint tomato juice (left over juice can be frozen in ice cube trays for future use)

salt and freshly ground black pepper

30 g/1 oz butter

1 tsp ground cumin

¹/₂ tsp ground coriander

1 green pepper, finely chopped

¹/₄ tsp dried chilli flakes (you can always add more to taste, but start small)

4 tbsp chopped fresh herbs such as parsley, coriander, mint

12 trimmed small lamb cutlets

1 tbsp sunflower oil

sprigs of mint to garnish

Preparation time: 15 minutes

Cooking time: 10 minutes

Serves: 4

Level of difficulty: 2

Drink suggestion: French medium red

1. Place the couscous into a large bowl. Bring the tomato juice to the boil, season with salt and freshly ground black pepper and pour it over the couscous. Add some extra boiling water to just cover the couscous, cover the bowl with clingfilm and leave for five minutes.

2. Melt the butter in a large pan and slowly fry the spices, add the chopped green pepper and as much of the dried chillies as you want, cook for another minute.

3. Fluff up the couscous with a fork and add it to the spices pan, stir gently, taste and season again, add the fresh herbs and keep warm.

4. Heat a griddle pan, frying pan or grill and season the lamb cutlets. Add oil to the pan and allow it to get quite hot but not smoking. Place the cutlets into the pan and cook each side for three minutes, until they are cooked but still pink in the centre.

5. Pile the couscous onto four plates, arrange the cutlets on top and add a sprig of mint for garnish.

spicy pork spare ribs

*Cooked in the oven or thrown on the
barbie, these tasty ribs won't last long.
Try and buy the meatiest ribs you can, or
if you prefer marinate cubes of pork or
chicken then thread onto a stick for
a kebab.*

Preparation time: 10 minutes

Cooking time: about 1 hour

Serves: 4

Level of difficulty: 1

Drink suggestion: medium red wine

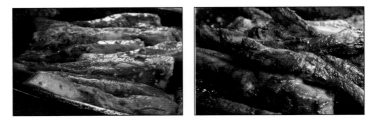

Ingredients

2 tsp sugar

salt and freshly ground black pepper

2 tbsp fresh orange juice

2 tbsp dark molasses/brown sugar

6 tbsp cider/white wine vinegar

1 tbsp tomato purée

4 garlic cloves, crushed

1 tsp ground cumin

1 tsp cayenne pepper

1 tsp paprika

1 tsp ground coriander

12 meaty pork spare ribs (3 per person)

1. In a large bowl, whisk all the ingredients except the ribs together to create the marinade. Cut the ribs into individual bones and place into the marinade. Cover and refrigerate for 24 hours. Placing the ribs and marinade into a strong plastic bag is a great way to marinate.

2. Preheat the oven to 200°C/400°F/gas mark 6. Transfer the ribs into a roasting tin, reserving any remaining marinade for basting. Bake for about an hour, or until very tender, basting regularly with a spoon or pastry brush and turning the ribs over.

3. Remove the ribs from the oven. They can be barbecued or grilled to finish them off with a really dark crust.

4. Eat with your fingers!

home-made pizza

The time and effort needed to make your own pizza dough may seem excessive but the results are worth it. This recipe makes a light, crispy base in keeping with the traditional pizzas you get in Italy.

Preparation time: 15 minutes, plus dough rising time of up to an hour

Cooking time: 10 minutes

Serves: 4

Level of difficulty: 2

Drink suggestion: Chianti

1. Line a bowl with olive oil and sift the flour and salt into it. Mix in the rosemary (if using), pepper, yeast and sugar. Add nearly all the water and mix to a soft dough with a knife. You may not need all the water.

2. Knead for five minutes on a floured surface. Place into a clean bowl and cover with clingfilm. Leave to rise in a warm place for 40 minutes or longer until double in size.

3. While the dough is rising, prepare the pizza toppings (see page 86 for ingredients). Tear or cut the ham, use a vegetable peeler to make Parmesan shavings, quarter the olives and so on.

4. Preheat the oven to 220°C/425°F/gas mark 7.

Ingredients
For the dough

450 g/1 lb strong plain flour

1 heaped tsp salt

1 tsp fresh rosemary, finely chopped (optional)

½ tsp cracked black pepper

7 g/ ½ tsp dried yeast (1 sachet)

½ tsp of sugar

300 ml/ ½ pint lukewarm water

olive oil for brushing

extra flour for kneading and shaping

(Ingredients continued on page 86)

5. Divide the dough into four pieces, shape into rounds and, with a rolling pin, roll each one as thinly as you can into a circle. Sprinkle flour over your baking trays to prevent sticking and transfer the dough bases. Leave them to rest just as long as it takes you to roll out the other bases, during which time they will shrink a little. Roll over each base again, while still on the tray, so that they are about 25 cm across.

(continued overleaf)

Ingredients (continued)

350 g/12 oz good-quality thick fresh tomato
sauce (1 jar)

200 g/7 oz grated mozzarella cheese

For your topping choose from:

4 slices thick cut parma or prosciutto ham, torn
into pieces (streaky bacon would work too)

30 g/1 oz Parmesan cheese for shavings

a handful of black olives

a few capers

a few anchovies

pepperoni slices

sliced peppers

12 sun-dried tomatoes, finely chopped

rocket or basil to garnish

6. To assemble the pizzas, take a large spoonful of the tomato sauce and spread thinly over the base, leaving a 2 cm margin around the edge.

7. Sprinkle over the mozzarella cheese and arrange the other topping ingredients over the pizza. Make sure there is not too much topping or the base will not cook.

8. Bake in the hot oven for about ten minutes or until the base is crisp and brown underneath.

9. Serve garnished with Parmesan shavings and some rocket.

Hot tip

If you don't have room in the oven to cook all the pizzas at once, they will hold, once made, for up to 30 minutes.

lemon, garlic & rosemary roast cod

Most fish has a delicate flavour so it's best to cook it simply – even the familiar cod can be turned into something special with only a few ingredients and the omission of batter!

Preparation time: 15 minutes

Cooking time: 15 minutes

Serves: 4

Level of difficulty: 1

Drink suggestion: dry French

Ingredients

120 ml/8 tbsp olive oil

8 cloves of garlic, with the skin still on

4 sprigs of rosemary

2 lemons, each cut into 6 wedges

4 thick pieces of cod fillet, about 170 g/6 oz each with the skin left on

1 tbsp plain flour, seasoned with salt and pepper

1. Preheat the oven to 200°C/400°F/gas mark 6.

2. Place the oil, garlic, rosemary and all but four of the lemon wedges in a roasting tin, squeezing the wedges as you put them in. Put in the oven for ten minutes to allow the oil to infuse. This can be done well in advance if you have time. Reheat for five minutes when you are ready to cook.

3. Check the fish for bones, leave the skin on and pat dry with kitchen paper. Dip the fish into the seasoned flour on the skin side only, shaking off the excess.

4. Remove the lemon, rosemary and garlic while you brown the fish, but do not discard.

5. Put the roasting tin directly on a hob. When the oil is hot carefully place in the seasoned fish, skin side down. When the skin side is golden brown turn the fillets, replace the lemon, rosemary and garlic and cook in the oven for 10–15 minutes or until the flesh is opaque and the flakes of fish begin to give when pressed. Serve with mashed potatoes (see page 94) and some roast tomatoes.

thai fish cakes

The comforts of a fish cake coupled with the heat and flavours of Thai cuisine, it's hard to beat.

Preparation time: 10 minutes

Cooking time: 10 minutes

Serves: 4 as a starter

Level of difficulty: 1

Drink suggestion: beer or dry Muscat wine

Ingredients

340 g/12 oz whiting or coley fillets, skinned and cut into chunks

$1/2$ a beaten egg

$1/2$ teaspoon brown sugar

2 tbsp fresh chopped coriander

1 kaffir lime leaf, finely shredded

$1/2$ tbsp Thai red curry paste, available at most supermarkets

$1/2$ tbsp Nam Pla (Thai fish sauce)

$1/2$ tsp salt

30 g/1 oz Thai long beans or French beans, finely chopped

2 tbsp sunflower oil

To serve

Thai sweet chilli dipping sauce

Fresh coriander sprigs

1. Check the fish thoroughly for bones then place the fillets with all the ingredients, except the beans and oil, into a food processor and blend until well mixed. Add the beans and pulse for only a second.

2. Divide and shape into four small cakes. You can use a large pastry cutter (see page 8) for this; just press the mixture into the cutter.

3. Heat the oil in a shallow pan and cook the fish cakes gently for four minutes on each side.

4. Serve with the sweet chilli sauce and garnish with fresh coriander.

Hot tip

As long as the fish is fresh these fish cakes can be frozen prior to cooking. Defrost thoroughly in the fridge and cook as above.

ultimate fish pie

By going to the fishmonger you can buy a fillet or a small chunk of any fish. If you say you want it for fish pie the fishmonger will help you make it up to 900 g/2 lb. You can use any combination of fish for your pie try getting haddock, salmon and a bit of smoked cod. Once you are a dab hand you can try adding scallops or prawns.

Preparation time and cooking time: about 1 hour

Serves: 4–6

Level of difficulty: 3

Drink suggestion: dry white wine

Ingredients

425 ml/ ³/₄ pint milk

¹/₂ onion sliced

6 black peppercorns

1 bay leaf

2 tbsp parsley – chop the leaves but leave the stalks whole

900 g/2 lb fish filets with skin on

30 g/1 oz butter

30 g/1 oz flour

salt and freshly ground black pepper

3 tbsp double cream (optional)

4 hard-boiled eggs (see page 37)

1.13 kg/2 ¹/₂ lb mashed potato, see page 94 for ingredients

To poach the fish

1. Preheat the oven to 180°C/350°F/gas mark 4.

2. Heat the milk in a roasting tin with the onion, peppercorns and bay leaf. If you have parsley stalks bash them and add to the milk.

3. Lay the fish fillets in the roasting tin, skin side up, cover with foil and cook in the oven for 15–20 minutes. (When you are using scallops and shellfish, add these for the last five minutes of the cooking time.)

4. When the fish is just cooked (see page 32) remove the skin from the fillets, checking for bones. Do this by tucking the prongs of a fork under the skin, gently twisting and rolling the skin around it (see picture above). With a fish slice remove the fish from the milk to a plate, remove the peppercorns and bay leaf, and sieve the milk to use for the sauce.

To make the white sauce

1. Heat the butter in a pan and add the flour, stir with a wooden spoon for two minutes. This is called a roux.

2. Now slowly add some of the milk (kept from poaching the fish) stirring all the time. The sauce will become thick and you should beat it steadily to remove any lumps. Slowly add the rest of the milk while continuing to stir.

3. Bring to the boil, stir for two minutes and taste. Season with salt and freshly ground black pepper.

4. Remove from the heat and add the double cream (if using) and chopped parsley.

mashed potatoes

Preparation time: 5 minutes	
Cooking time: 20 minutes	
Level of difficulty: 1	
Serves: 4	

Ingredients

900 g/2 lb maris piper potatoes, washed, peeled and cut into even-sized chunks

2 tsp salt

300 ml/ ½ pint creamy milk

55 g/2 oz unsalted butter

salt and freshly ground black pepper

To make the mashed potato

1. Place the prepared potatoes in a large pan of cold water. Add the salt and bring to the boil. Cover with a lid and simmer until the potatoes are tender (about 15 minutes – test with a cutlery knife, it should sink into the potato when it's cooked).

2. Drain the potatoes in a colander and place back into the pan. Pour most of the milk into the pan and heat gently with the butter. Once steaming, mash with a potato masher and then season well with salt and freshly ground black pepper. Take care not to over stir the potato as it can go gluey. Add more milk if it is too firm. Delicious!

To assemble the pie

1. Place the fish into a large shallow ovenproof dish with the quartered hard-boiled eggs and pour the sauce evenly over the top. Stir if necessary but do this gently.

2. Spread or pipe (see page 9) the the potato on top. Return it to the oven to heat through (see reheating information below). If all the ingredients are already hot it can just be flashed under the grill to brown the potato.

Hot tip

This pie freezes well so you can make two and freeze one. Allow to defrost in the fridge overnight and reheat for 30–60 minutes at 190°C/375°F/gas mark 5 depending on the size of the pie, always check the pie is thoroughly heated all the way through.

chilli & parsley pesto with barbecued tuna

Pesto is traditionally made with basil but this recipe substitutes parsley a herb that complements the flavours of the tuna steak perfectly, the added chillies give a great kick too. You will need a blender for this recipe, but if the weather isn't up to barbecue then cook the tuna in a griddle or frying pan.

Preparation time: 20 minutes	
Cooking time: 5 minutes	
Serves: 4	
Level of difficulty: 2	
Drink suggestion: Sauvignon Blanc	

Ingredients

4 thick tuna steaks, about 6 oz/170 g

1 tbsp olive oil (for pan frying and griddling)

For the pesto

a large bunch of flat leaf parsley, stalks removed

2 green chillies

$^1/_2$ clove of garlic, bashed and peeled

1 tbsp pine nuts or almonds

7 tbsp olive oil

2 tbsp grated Parmesan cheese (optional)

salt and freshly ground black pepper

To make the pesto

1. Wash and roughly chop the parsley. Remove the stalk from the chillies, slice in half lengthways and remove the seeds if you don't want the pesto to be extra hot. Roughly chop the flesh of the chilli (see page 21).

2. Place the parsley and chillies into a blender with the garlic. Blend for two minutes then add the nuts and oil. You may have to turn the machine off to poke the mixture down with a spoon a couple of times as it does tend to stick. When it looks combined add the cheese and season with salt and freshly ground black pepper. Store in the fridge in a sealed container such as a jam jar. The pesto will stay green for at least two weeks.

Hot tip

If you want to make the pesto more of a sauce, just add some water when making it and it will emulsify like mayonnaise, giving you a bright green smooth sauce.

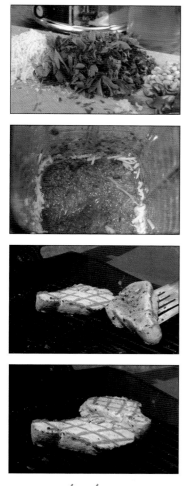

To cook the tuna

1. Preheat the barbecue or grill.

2. Brush the tuna steaks with a little olive oil and season with salt and freshly ground black pepper. Place on the hottest part of the barbecue and leave for at least three minutes.

3. Use a fish slice or pallet knife to gently turn the steaks. They should not stick if the barbecue is really hot. Cook for another three minutes and transfer to serving plates and accompany with the pesto. Serve with chunky chips (page 114).

quick mushroom soup

A simple soup, full of flavour and a far cry from the 'cream of' varieties stacked high in the supermarket.

A note about cooking with cream

Single cream normally contains about 18 per cent fat and must not be boiled. When using it for soups or sauces it should be added at the end of cooking and carefully reheated. Double cream has about 48 per cent fat and is stable enough to be boiled. It is perfect for sauces that are made by reducing down the flavours to make them more intense. If you want something less rich in flavour try crème fraîche which is also high in fat and can be boiled. If using one that is low in fat (such as half fat crème fraîche) treat it like single cream.

Preparation time: 10 minutes

Cooking time: 30 minutes

Serves: 4

Level of difficulty: 1

Drink suggestion: light dry white wine

Ingredients

30 g/1 oz butter

1 small onion, finely chopped

1 small garlic clove, chopped

450 g/1 lb mushrooms, (preferably flat caps) chopped

1 slice of bread, crusts removed

1 litre/1¾ pints chicken or vegetable stock

salt and freshly ground black pepper

a pinch of nutmeg

parsley stalks bashed and tied with kitchen string

2 tbsp fresh chopped parsley (for garnish)

single cream (optional)

1. Melt the butter in a large heavy-based saucepan. Add the onion, sweat (cook gently without colouring the onions) for ten minutes.

2. Add the garlic and the mushrooms and cook slowly for ten minutes, stirring while they soften. Crumble in the bread and stir again to combine.

3. Add the stock, seasoning, nutmeg and tied parsley stalks (this way you get the flavour without annoying bits of stalk) and bring to the boil. Simmer for ten minutes.

4. Remove the parsley stalks and string, liquidise and sieve the soup if you want. This is not necessary if you want a rustic finish.

5. When you are ready to serve, re-heat the soup, garnish with parsley and finish with a little cream.

spinach & blue cheese pasta

A classic combination of flavours that's even easier than spag bol to cook!

A note on cooking pasta

To check whether pasta is cooked you can simply eat a bit. It should feel cooked but not chewy. Alternatively you can cut a piece in half and it won't have a white, starchy middle once it's cooked.

Preparation time: 10 minutes

Cooking time: 15 minutes

Serves: 4

Level of difficulty: 1

Drink suggestion: Italian dry white or light Italian red

Ingredients

1 tsp salt

340 g/12 oz dried pasta, tagliatelle, tubes or twists (allow 85 g/3 oz of dried pasta per person)

4 tbsp olive oil

2 small onions, finely chopped

2 garlic cloves, crushed

170 g/6 oz frozen spinach or 340 g/12 oz fresh spinach

4 tbsp crème fraîche

170 g/6 oz blue cheese, such as Dolcelatte or Gorgonzola, cut into cubes

salt and freshly ground black pepper

1. Bring a large pan of water to the boil. Add a teaspoon of salt and cook the pasta according to the instructions on the packet. It should be al denté, which means soft, but retaining a slight bite to the teeth (see the note above).

2. While the pasta is cooking, heat the oil in a shallow pan and cook the onion and garlic gently for a few minutes. Remove to a plate.

3. Add the spinach to the pan and cook until it thaws out or wilts. If using fresh spinach you will need to drain and squeeze it before continuing.

4. Return the onion and garlic to the pan and add the crème fraîche and blue cheese.

5. Add the cooked, drained pasta to the pan. Mix well, taste and season with salt and freshly ground black pepper. Serve immediately.

sun-dried &
cherry tomato risotto

Risotto is an often overlooked Italian dish but it's a great alternative to pasta and this dish makes a satisfying meat-free meal.

Preparation time: 20 minutes

Cooking time: 40 minutes

Serves: 4

Level of difficulty: 2

Drink suggestion: Australian Shiraz/Italian red

Ingredients

1.70 litres/3 pints vegetable stock

85 g/3 oz sun-dried tomatoes, chopped

55 g/2 oz butter

1 tbsp olive oil

2 small red onions, chopped

2 small garlic cloves, crushed

400 g/14 oz arborio (risotto) rice

1 tbsp bought pesto sauce (optional)

110 g/4 oz oyster or field mushrooms, sliced

salt and freshly ground black pepper

225 g/8 oz cherry tomatoes, washed

55 g/2 oz Parmesan cheese

chopped fresh flat-leaf parsley, to garnish

1. In a large saucepan, heat the vegetable stock with the sun-dried tomatoes over a medium heat.

2. Heat the butter and oil in another large pan. Add the onions and garlic and cook, stirring occasionally for five minutes, or until soft.

3. Add the rice and cook, stirring, for one minute. Add the pesto sauce (if using) and cook for three or four further minutes. Begin to add the stock, a ladleful at a time, bring to a simmer, stirring occasionally, until the liquid has been absorbed. Continue slowly adding the stock, allowing it to be absorbed in between.

4. Stir in the mushrooms and season with salt and pepper. Simmer until all the liquid has been absorbed and the rice is tender and creamy. You may need to add a little more stock. It should take about 30 minutes for the rice to cook, add the tomatoes to heat through in the last five minutes of cooking.

5. Using a vegetable peeler, shave curls of Parmesan cheese over the risotto, sprinkle with parsley and serve.

vegetable curry
with lemon-scented rice

A satisfying curry that's great as a main course or side dish.

Preparation time: 30 minutes

Cooking time: 30 minutes

Serves: 2 as a main dish or 4 as a side dish

Level of difficulty: 2

Drink suggestion: Indian Beer

Ingredients

1 tbsp sunflower oil

1 red onion, sliced

1 carrot, peeled and finely diced

2 garlic cloves, crushed

225 g/8 oz potatoes, peeled and diced

1 tbsp medium curry paste (adjust to taste)

1/2 tsp ground coriander

1 tsp peeled and grated fresh ginger

400 g/14 oz tinned chopped tomatoes (1 tin)

400 g/14 oz tinned chickpeas, drained (1 tin)

150 ml/ 1/4 pint vegetable stock

salt and freshly ground black pepper

a small handful fresh coriander, chopped

For the rice

55 g/2 oz uncooked basmati rice per person

zest of two lemons

fresh coriander chopped

1. Heat the oil in a large saucepan. Add the onion, carrot and garlic and cook on a low heat for ten minutes with a lid on. Add the potatoes, curry paste, ground coriander and ginger and cook, stirring, for a further five minutes.

2. Add the tomatoes, chickpeas and vegetable stock, bring to the boil and cook uncovered for 15 minutes, stirring every few minutes to make sure it doesn't stick.

3. Check the potatoes are tender and season with salt and freshly ground black pepper. If you think the curry is too dry, add a little stock or water. If too wet, boil rapidly to evaporate any excess liquid. Add the fresh coriander and serve with naan bread and/or lemon-scented rice.

To cook the rice

1. Wash the rice in cold water, using a sieve, rinse until the water runs clear.

2. Place the rice into a large pan of boiling salted water (about one teaspoon of salt per 110 g/4 oz rice). As the water returns to the boil stir once and turn down to a low simmer so that the water is just moving gently.

3. Leave uncovered. Cook for 8–10 minutes and test by eating a bit. It should feel tender and, like pasta, if you cut a grain in half it should have no white starch visible in the middle.

4. Once cooked, strain into a sieve or fine colander. Leave to steam over the pan for a few minutes, then fork through it gently to prevent the grains sticking together.

5. Using the fine side of a grater, grate the peel of the lemon – try not to press too hard so you pull the pith (white bit) away. Add the zest (peel) and stir through the rice adding the chopped coriander.

red onion omelette

This recipe is delicious as a breakfast, starter or light meal and it's fantastic hot or cold. Once cooked it can be kept in the fridge for up to a day. You will need a 23 cm/9 in. non-stick omelette or frying pan; if making this for two people use a 14 cm/6 in. pan and half the ingredients.

Preparation time: 15 minutes

Cooking time: 30 minutes

Serves: 4

Level of difficulty: 1

Drink suggestion: Côtes-du-Rhone

Ingredients

1 tbsp olive oil

30 g/1 oz butter

3 large red onions, peeled, halved and sliced

6 eggs

salt and freshly ground black pepper

a good pinch of paprika

55 g/2 oz Parmesan cheese, grated

1. Heat the oil and butter on a medium heat in the non-stick frying pan.

2. Add the sliced onions, stir and cover with a plate or lid. Lower the heat and cook slowly until soft, stirring occasionally. This is called sweating and will take about 15 minutes.

3. Meanwhile, crack the eggs into a bowl and season with salt, pepper and paprika.

4. Add the Parmesan cheese and beat with a small whisk or fork until well mixed. Once the onions are soft pour the egg mix onto the onions and turn the heat right down.

5. Cook very slowly for 15 minutes; the eggs should be set and the surface slightly runny.

6. Place the pan under a preheated hot grill for a few minutes to brown the top. It will feel firm when cooked.

7. Slide onto a plate and serve cut into wedges.

welsh rarebit

For a light lunch or a top snack to enjoy with the game, you can't beat a bit of cheese on toast and this recipe is the ultimate version of a great classic, enjoy!

Preparation time: 10 minutes

Cooking time: 5 minutes

Serves: 4

Level of difficulty: 1

Drink suggestion: light red wine

1. Preheat the grill.

2. Combine the first six ingredients.

3. Place the bread on a baking sheet and toast lightly on both sides. Spread with butter.

4. Spoon the cheese mix onto each slice of bread right up to the edges.

5. Place under the grill and cook until nicely browned and set, cut into fingers and serve at once.

Ingredients

85 g/3 oz Gruyère cheese, grated

85 g/3 oz mature cheddar cheese, grated

3 tsp French mustard

salt and freshly ground black pepper

1 egg, beaten

4 tbsp beer

4 slices of bread

butter for spreading

Hot tip

For fancy Welsh rarebit you can use a soft blue cheese along with the Gruyère, or stick to the recipe given here but spread a little chutney onto the bread before placing the cheese mix on top.

egg & bacon quiche

Real men do eat quiche and the easiest way to make this quiche is to buy a pre-baked pastry case and simply follow the recipe below. For the more adventurous cook I've also explained how to make shortcrust pastry and how to roll and line a flan tin, so there are no excuses.

Preparation time: 20 minutes

Cooking time: 30 minutes

Serves: 4

Level of difficulty: 2 (3 if you use bought raw pastry or make your own)

Drink suggestion: white Alsace wine

Ingredients

15 g/ ½ oz butter

1 medium onion, finely chopped

110 g/4 oz rindless bacon, cut into small dice

2 eggs

5 tbsp milk

150 ml/ ¼ pint single cream

55 g/2 oz mature cheddar cheese, grated on the small side of a grater

freshly ground black pepper

20 cm/8 in. cooked pastry case (or see pages 112–113 for how to make your own)

1. Preheat the oven to 150°C/300°F/gas mark 2. Melt the butter in a small pan, over a medium heat, and cook the onion with a lid until soft – about 15 minutes. In another pan fry the bacon until slightly crispy (you don't need oil for this). Place both in a sieve to drain and cool while you make the egg mixture.

2. Whisk the eggs until well mixed and then add the milk, cream and cheese, mix well and season with freshly ground black pepper (the cheese and bacon should provide enough salt).

3. Add the onion and bacon and pour the mix into the baked pastry case. If you have any mix leftover after filling the pastry case you can cook it in a ramekin (a small ceramic dish often used to cook souffles) in the oven in the same way.

4. Place the quiche into the lower part of the oven and cook for about 30 minutes. The quiche should be set and not too brown. If it starts to puff up remove it from the oven as it is beginning to over cook. Serve hot or cold.

shortcrust pastry

If your feeling confident in your skills why not try rolling out bought pastry or even making your own? Prepare and cook your pastry case as follows then continue with the recipe as outlined on the previous page.

Ingredients

85 g/3 oz butter

170 g/6 oz plain flour

pinch of salt

1 egg yolk mixed with 3 tbsp of water

To make shortcrust pastry

1. Preheat oven to 200°C/400°F/gas mark 6. Freeze the butter for an hour – if you have time – then grate it and quickly re-freeze so it doesn't melt.

2. Sift the flour into a bowl with a pinch of salt. Stir in the butter using a knife, then, using your fingertips, gently rub the butter through the flour. Do not allow it to go yellow; this means the butter is warming up too much.

3. When the mix resembles breadcrumbs add in half the mixed yolk and water, stir with the knife and see if the pastry will come together. Use your hand to bring it together. Add a little more liquid if necessary. Shape into a flatish ball, cover and chill for 20 minutes.

4. Alternatively, you can place the flour, salt and the chopped up butter into a food processor. Then process the mixture until it resembles breadcrumbs; rub some between your finger and thumb to ensure the butter is well blended. Again, do not allow it to go yellow. Put the mixture into a bowl, add in the egg and water. Use your hand to bring it together. Add a little more liquid if necessary. Shape into a flatish ball cover and chill for 20 minutes (1).

To roll out fresh pastry

1. Roll the pastry out an inch or so larger than the flan tin (you will need a 20 cm/ 8 in. flan case) about 5 mm thick (2). If your pastry was bought frozen or was very chilled allow to defrost to room temperature before rolling.

2. Use the rolling pin to help you lift the pastry and position it in the tin as neatly as you can (3–5). Roll off with the pin (roll it over the top of the flan tin so the overhanging pastry is cut away) and tidy the edge (6 & 7). Patch up any holes with the leftover pastry to stop the liquid filling escaping.

3. Chill for another 20 minutes.

Hot tip
Uncooked pastry freezes really well, either store in a ball or freeze the pastry case in the tin.

To bake blind

1. Preheat the oven to 200°C/400°F/gas mark 6. Protect the pastry with a circle of greaseproof paper and place baking beans or baking weights in the centre (8). (Baking weights can be obtained from any kitchen shop. Alternatively you can use lentils or other dried pulses. These prevent the pastry from puffing up and bubbling.)

2. Place the flan tin on a baking sheet and cook in the top of the oven for ten minutes. Remove the beans and paper and return the tin to the oven for another ten minutes (on a lower shelf) or until the pastry is dried out but not coloured (9). The pastry is then ready for its filling, in most cases it doesn't need to be cool before the filling is added but check the recipe.

chunky, healthy chips

These chunky, wedge chips are great as a snack on their own or to serve with any number of dishes, especially a home-made burger (page 54) or steak sandwich (page 62).

Preparation time: 5 minutes

Cooking time: 25–35 minutes

Level of difficulty: 1

Serves: 4

Drink suggestion: light red wine/beer

1. Preheat the oven to 200°C/400°F/gas mark 6. Wash the potatoes and cut each one into 6–8 wedges – leave the skins on.

2. Place the wedges into a plastic or glass bowl with an inch of water, cover with a plate and microwave for 5–10 minutes so that a knife just penetrates the potatoes. Carefully check after seven minutes to see how they are doing.

3. Heat the olive oil in a roasting tin and add the potatoes, coat in the oil, adding the garlic and herbs if using (see hot tip), and roast in the oven for 20–30 minutes or until deep golden brown and crisp. Drain on kitchen paper and season with salt and pepper.

Ingredients

4 large potatoes (1 per person) cara, desirée or King Edward

4 tbsp olive oil (1 tbsp per potato)

salt and pepper

Hot tip

Crushed garlic left in its papery skin and herbs (particularly rosemary and thyme), make tasty additions to these chips. Add the herbs and garlic as the potatoes go into the oven.

garlic baked new potatoes

This method of cooking in a bag is called en papillote. Any quick cooked item can be done in this way. Try cooking a piece of fish instead of the potatoes, it will only take about ten minutes. Fruit can also be cooked this way, try bananas and apricots wrapped in foil.

Preparation time: 5 minutes

Cooking time: 45 minutes to 1 hour

Serves: 4

Level of difficulty: 1

Drink suggestion: light red

1. Preheat the oven to 200°C/400°F/gas mark 6. Cut two large heart shapes from greaseproof paper, each half of the heart should be at least as large as an A4 piece of paper, 21 cm × 30 cm.

2. Divide the potatoes into two lots, place a pile of potatoes and two unpeeled garlic cloves onto one side of each heart shape.

3. Drizzle each with half the oil, season with salt and freshly ground black pepper and add the thyme and rosemary.

4. Fold the heart in half and starting with the rounded top edge begin to make small folds to seal the edges of the paper. One fold should secure the previous fold. Finish with a twist at the point.

5. Place on a baking sheet (you may need two sheets if the parcels are too big) and bake for about 45 minutes to an hour. Test they are done by poking the potatoes through the paper with a skewer. The potatoes will brown beautifully through the paper, and you can serve straight from the paper.

Ingredients

750 g/1 lb 10 oz new potatoes, washed

4 garlic cloves

4 tsp olive oil

salt and freshly ground black pepper

2 sprigs thyme, very finely chopped

2 springs rosemary

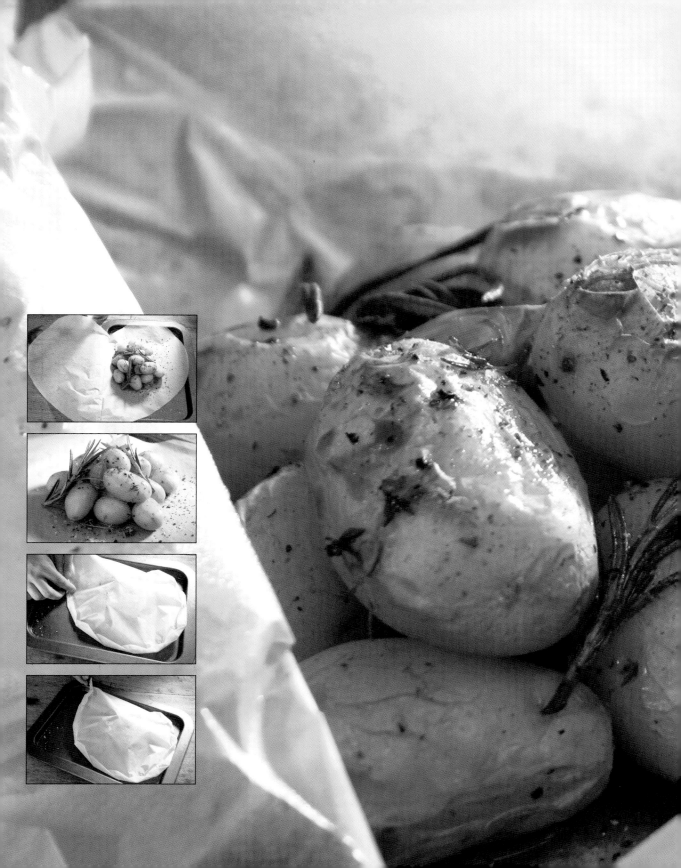

roasted vegetables

Roasting is such an easy way to serve vegetables, a one-tray wonder which vegetarians and meat eaters alike will love.

Preparation time: 15 minutes

Cooking time: 1 hour

Level of difficulty: 1

Drink suggestion: light Red

Ingredients

Allow about 900 g/2 lb total weight of vegetables for 4 people

Choose from: firm, slow-cooked vegetables; carrots, celery, new potatoes, swede, turnip, leek, or baby onions. Softer quicker-cooked vegetables; aubergine, courgettes, celeriac, parsnip, Brussels sprouts, butternut squash or sweet potato.

Olive oil

Thyme and rosemary sprigs

Salt and freshly ground black pepper

1. Preheat the oven to 200°C/400°F/gas mark 6. Choose a combination of the listed vegetables, wash, peel and cut into large cubes, about the size of a small Brussels sprout.

2. Place the firm vegetables into a roasting tin with a few tablespoons of olive oil, herbs, salt and freshly ground black pepper, stir well. Cover with foil and place on the top shelf of the oven.

3. After 20 minutes add the prepared softer vegetables, stir carefully and return to the oven without the foil. Cook for another half an hour and stir carefully twice during the cooking time. Check the vegetables are tender and slightly caramelised.

4. Serve with any roast dinner or your favourite main course.

Hot tip

Cubes of bacon are delicious cooked with vegetables. The addition of herbs, such as thyme and rosemary, will also give a wonderful aromatic flavour. Alternatively, add some honey towards the end of the cooking time and return to the oven for a really golden, mouth-watering finish.

hot potato salad

Everyone is familiar with the cold, mayonnaise-covered potato salad but this hot version is more delicious and versatile when served with different dressings to suit your main course.

Preparation time: 5 minutes	
Cooking time: 20 minutes	
Serves: 4	
Level of difficulty: 1	
Drink suggestion: beer	

Ingredients

450 g/1 lb washed new potatoes or peeled old potatoes, cut into even-sized pieces. Allow 110 g/4 oz potatoes per person

a good pinch of salt

chopped herbs of choice, such as fennel, dill, basil, chives, mint or oregano

salt and freshly ground black pepper

Use one of these three dressings:

1) 4 tbsp olive oil and 1$\frac{1}{2}$ tbsp balsamic vinegar and seasoning

2) 4 tbsp bought mayonnaise mixed with grainy, French or Dijon mustard

3) 4 tbsp olive oil and 2 tbsp chilli vinegar

1. Place the potatoes in enough salted water to cover them; new potatoes usually go into boiling water, but cold will do.

2. Bring them up to the boil and simmer with a lid until tender – about 20 minutes. Test them with a knife and drain in a colander. Leave them to steam while you make the dressing.

3. Mix your choice of dressing and pour over the potatoes while still hot, season with salt and freshly ground black pepper. Add any chopped soft-leaf herbs, serve at once.

Note
The mayonnaise-based dressed potatoes must be eaten straight away but the oil and vinegar dressed potatoes can be left in the fridge overnight for a cold salad.

pancakes with flambéed bananas

You can make the pancakes in advance as they freeze well. When you are ready to serve, warm the pancakes in a microwave or wrapped in foil and heat in a low oven.

Preparation time: 10 minutes for the batter

Cooking time: 20 minutes to make the pancakes and 5 minutes for the flambé

Serves: 4

Level of difficulty: 2

Drink suggestion: rum

Ingredients

Makes 290 ml of batter or 8–10 pancakes, depending on how large your pan is and how thick you like your pancakes.

For the batter

110 g/4 oz plain flour

pinch of salt

2 eggs, beaten

300 ml/ ½ pint semi-skimmed milk

1 tsp sunflower oil

oil for cooking and a piece of kitchen paper

To make the batter

1. In a large bowl sift the flour and salt. Using a wooden spoon make a hole in the centre.

2. Crack the eggs into the hole and, working in a small circular motion, begin to incorporate the flour. When half the flour is mixed in begin to add a little of the milk.

3. All of the flour should be mixed in by the time half the milk is added. Beat or whisk the batter to make it smooth and lump-free, then add the remaining milk and the teaspoon of oil.

4. Sieve the batter if it contains any lumps and chill for 30 minutes.

To cook the pancakes

1. Heat a non-stick frying pan or skillet over a medium-high heat. Wipe it with a piece of oiled kitchen paper. Test that the pan is hot enough by dripping a bit of batter onto the base of the pan. It should cook and become unstuck at once. Remove it and start to make your pancakes.

2. Pour a little batter into the pan and quickly swill it round to cover the base of the pan.

3. Allow it to cook and tease the edges with a pallet or cutlery knife to see if they come away.

4. Turn the pancake when you can get the knife underneath, or toss them if you're feeling brave. Cook for a minute or so on the other side and turn out onto a warmed plate.

5. Wipe the pan with the oiled kitchen paper between pancakes and stack them all on a warmed plate as you make them.

Hot tip

Pancakes can be cooked and layered with a strip of greaseproof paper between each one. They can then be placed in bags and frozen. One or two pancakes can be defrosted whenever you fancy a quick pudding. Pancakes   are also great for a quick starter or main course; just fill with chilli, avocado and sour cream — or whatever takes your fancy.

For the banana flambé

30 g/1 oz unsalted butter

4 small firm bananas, cut into thick, slanted rounds

a pinch of cinnamon

30 g/1 oz light muscovado sugar

juice of 1 lime

2 tbsp light rum

vanilla ice cream, to serve

For the flambé

1. Over a fairly high heat, melt the butter in a heavy-based frying pan. Add the bananas and cook, tossing constantly until lightly golden.

2. Sprinkle over the cinnamon and sugar. Continue to cook for another minute or so until the bananas have just begun to caramelise.

3. Pour the lime juice into the pan and cook for another 1–2 minutes or until the bananas are completely tender but still holding their shape.

4. Heat the rum in a small pan or ladle. Set it alight by tipping towards the gas flame or using a lit taper. Pour carefully over the bananas, shake the pan gently and allow the flames to die down.

5. Fill the pancakes with the bananas, roll up or fold in quarters and serve with vanilla ice cream.

easy chocolate mousse

This recipe is a synch; it just involves being organised and then going for it. The crème fraîche in this recipe gives this mousse a more adult flavour, but you can use extra thick double cream if you prefer.

Preparation time: 20 minutes

Chilling time: 2 hours

Serves: 4–5

Level of difficulty: 2

Drink suggestion: Orange Muscat or Madeira

Ingredients

140 g/5 oz good quality dark chocolate, broken up into chunks

2 eggs

150 ml/ ^{1}/$_4$ pt crème fraîche

1. Melt the chocolate in a bowl placed over a saucepan of steaming water, known as a bain-marie. Alternatively you can melt it in the microwave on the defrost setting. It will take about five minutes and you need to stop and stir every minute or so.

2. Remove the chocolate from the heat as the last few lumps melt. This prevents the chocolate becoming overheated which can leave it looking dry and lumpy. Allow to cool.

3. Separate the eggs, putting the whites into a larger bowl, the yolks into a cup.

4. When the chocolate is cool, but not setting, whisk the egg white until it just holds its shape – about five minutes with a hand-held non-electric whisk.

5. Still using your whisk, but with a stirring movement rather than a whisking movement, add the yolks to the chocolate and stir briskly for 15 seconds. Add the crème fraîche and stir for a further 30 seconds.

6. Add half the whisked egg white, stirring in. Then add the remaining egg white and gently fold it in until mixed.

7. Place into glasses, ramekins or a medium-sized bowl and freeze for 30 minutes, or leave for a few hours in the fridge. Serve with posh biscuits.

Hot tip

When melting chocolate, even a drop of water can make it stiff and lumpy, so be careful. If the chocolate has gone really lumpy you can add a knob of butter and blend it in. This should make it smooth again and allow you to continue with the recipe. The same applies if the chocolate is overheated and goes dry and grainy.

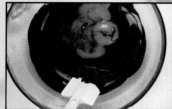

summer fruit pavlova

*A classic pudding that won't fail to impress. I've
used blueberries in this example but you could
use any berry in season, raspberries are
particularly good.*

Preparation time: 25 minutes

Cooking time: 1 hour

Serves: 4

Level of difficulty: 2

Drink suggestion: muscatel/sweet sherry

until the egg whites become fluffy and an opaque white and
form soft peaks when you lift the beaters up.

Ingredients

2 egg whites

110 g/4 oz caster sugar

$1/2$ teaspoon cornflour

$1/2$ teaspoon white wine vinegar

A few drops of vanilla essence

200 ml/ $1/3$ pint double cream

300 g/ $10^{1}/2$ raspberries or blueberries

4 sprigs fresh mint

1. Preheat the oven to 130°C/250°F/ gas mark $1/2$.
Line a baking sheet with a piece of non-stick
baking parchment.

2. Using an electric whisk, whisk the egg whites in
a very clean bowl (any grease residue on the
bowl will prevent the whites stiffening). Whisk

3. Now start to slowly add the caster sugar as you continue
to whisk, the mix should begin to become stiff and very shiny.
Continue to add the sugar in stages; by the end you should
be able to stand a teaspoon up in the mixture.

4. Whisk in the vinegar, cornflour and vanilla.

5. Using a metal spoon or plastic spatula, transfer the mixture
onto the baking sheet, spreading it out into a circle. Bake on
the lowest shelf for about 45 minutes or until the meringue
comes cleanly away from the paper. Remember that meringue
is supposed to be soft and gooey in the middle. Allow to cool;
it can be kept for a few days at this stage.

6. Whip the cream until it holds its shape. Spoon the cream
into the middle of the meringue. Pile the blueberries on top
of the cream, and garnish with a sprig of mint.

Note

*This recipe will make four small individual pavlovas, Just spoon four oval shapes
onto the baking sheet and make a small dip in the centre of each. Cook at the
same temperature for 45 mins or until the meringue comes cleanly off the paper.*

mixed berry frozen yoghurt

Desserts don't come much easier than this all you need is a working food processor and an index finger! Don't defrost the berries, you'll end up with a watery mush, use them straight from the freezer. The other thing about this recipe is that it's relatively diet-friendly, especially if you use half-fat Greek yoghurt.

Preparation time: 15 minutes

Serves: 4

Level of difficulty: 1

Drink suggestion: crème de cassis/ raspberry liqueur

Ingredients

225 g/8 oz mixed frozen summer fruits

450 g/1 lb Greek yoghurt

3 tbsp cranberry and raspberry juice

1. Place all the ingredients into a food processor and whiz until everything is mixed. You may need to scrape the sides a few times to incorporate all the berries.

2. Serve straight away in iced glasses, or you can keep in the freezer for up to two hours.

mascarpone & white chocolate cheesecake with berries

Ingredients
For the biscuit crust

200 g/7 oz digestive biscuits (about 12 biscuits)

55 g/2 oz butter

For the filling

170 g/6 oz white chocolate, broken into pieces

250 g/9 oz mascarpone cheese

1 tbsp orange or cherry liqueur

200 ml/ 7 fl oz crème fraîche (low fat is fine)

1 large punnet (about 200 g/7 oz) of red berries such as strawberries or raspberries. Use more or less according to taste

mint to garnish

Hot tip
To remove the tin, wear rubber gloves and dip a clean cloth into very hot water, wring out the cloth and place it around the outside of the tin. The tin will warm up and you can slide it off. You can also make individual cheesecakes (as pictured) using pastry cutters or a muffin tin lined with clingfilm.

Preparation time: 20 minutes
Chilling time: 1 hour
Serves: 6
Level of difficulty: 2
Drink suggestion: sweet sparkling wine

1. Place the biscuits in a large food bag and crush with a rolling pin until they resemble breadcrumbs.

2. Melt the butter in a pan and add the crushed biscuits. Mix well and using a spoon, push tightly into the base of a shallow 20 cm/8 in. loose-bottomed cake tin or flan ring. Chill in the fridge while you make the topping.

3. Put the chocolate and mascarpone into a glass bowl over a pan of barely simmering water. Stir to melt the chocolate and as the last few lumps are melting remove from the heat and stir until smooth. Stir in the liqueur then leave to cool slightly.

4. Stir the crème fraîche into the cooled chocolate mixture. Pour onto the biscuit base and leave to set in the fridge for about an hour.

5. Remove the cake tin or flan ring and serve piled with the berries. Garnish with mint.

chocolate sandwich cake

*Your reportoire wouldn't be complete
without a good birthday cake!*

Preparation time: 30 minutes

Cooking time: 30 minutes

Serves: 6–8

Level of difficulty: 1

Drink suggestion: sweet sherry/ Madeira

Ingredients

oil (sunflower or vegetable) for greasing

roll of parchment paper

225 g/8 oz butter, kept at room temperature

225 g/8 oz caster sugar

4 large free range eggs

200 g/7 oz self-raising flour, sifted

a large pinch of baking powder

30 g/1 oz cocoa powder

150 ml/ ¼ pint double cream, whipped

fresh raspberries optional

1. Preheat the oven to 180°C/375°F/gas mark 4.
Prepare two 20 cm/8 in. sandwich tins and line
each one with parchment paper.

2. With an electric whisk, cream (beat) the
butter with the sugar until pale and fluffy. Beat
the eggs and add them slowly to the creamed
mixture, blending well between each addition.

3. Fold in the sifted flour, baking powder and
cocoa. Add a tiny bit of water to bring the
mixture to a dropping consistency.

4. Place the mixture into the prepared tins. Bake in the oven
for 25 minutes or until the mixture springs back when lightly
pressed with a fingertip. Remove from the oven and allow to
cool in the tins. Once cool, remove from the tins and discard
the lining paper. Sandwich together with the cream or even
crème fraîche. Dust with caster sugar. Alternatively, sandwich
with a layer of cream, chocolate icing (see below) and fresh
raspberries, top with the chocolate icing as pictured.

To make a delicious chocolate icing

Place 150 ml/ ¼ pt double cream in a small pan and bring to the
boil. Break up or grate 110 g/4 oz good quality cooking chocolate
into a bowl. When the cream comes to the boil (see notes on
page 99), remove from the heat and add the chocolate. Stir until
melted and allow to cool slightly before spreading onto your cake.
The icing will thicken as it cools so put it on the cake before it
sets! This quantity is enough to fill the cake as well as ice it, or you
can make the extra into truffles or freeze it. Just warm it in the
microwave on the defrost setting to melt it for your next cake.

Hot tip

*For a quicker cake, place all the ingredients (except the cream) into a
food processor and whiz until blended, then bake as usual. It may not
be as light as the creamed cake but not many will notice.*

menu suggestions

The beauty of being able to cook a number of different recipes is that you can combine them according to the occasion. Here are a few ideas about which dishes to put with which. These are only suggestions, and you can mix and match according to your preference. Equally – if you feel overawed by producing more than one dish for an event – you could concentrate on just producing one course using a recipe from this book, and buy in any other courses.

dinner party

STARTER	Warm chicken salad
MAIN COURSE	Spicy lamb cutlets or lemon roast cod
DESSERT	Easy chocolate mousse

What to do in advance
- Chicken can be rolled in flour in advance and chilled
- Salad can be washed, but not dressed
- Dressing can be made
- The couscous can be cooked, ready to be reheated in the microwave with the herbs
- The chocolate mousse can be made a few hours before or even the day before

On the night
- Fry the chicken, dress the salad
- Fry the cutlets or roast the cod
- Cook accompanying potatoes/vegetables

romantic dinner

STARTER	Welsh rarebit
MAIN COURSE	Chicken breasts with shitake noodles
DESSERT	Mascarpone & white chocolate cheesecake

What to do in advance
- The mix for the rarebit can be made up and kept in the fridge
- The chicken can be marinated the day before; all the ingredients for the noodles can be prepared in advance
- The cheesecake can be made the day before

On the night
- Prepare and cook the rarebit
- Cook the chicken breasts with shitake noodles

friends for the footy

MAIN COURSE	Spicy sausage and chickpea soup or beef chilli

What to do in advance

- Either the soup or the chilli can be made in advance

On the night

- Cook the rice and reheat the chilli
- Or heat through the soup and serve it with lots of crusty bread

barbecue

BUFFET	Tuna with chilli pesto
	Home-made beef burgers
	Spicy pork spare ribs
	Hot potato salad
	Leaf salad
	Summer fruit Pavlova

What to do in advance

- Make the pesto
- Marinate the spare ribs
- Wash the salad
- Make the burgers
- Cook the meringue

On the night

- Cook the potatoes and dress
- Cook the tuna, burgers and spare ribs on the barbecue
- Dress the salad
- Add the whipped cream and fruit to the Pavlova

cooking for veggies

STARTER	Red onion omelette
MAIN COURSE	Sun-dried tomato risotto
DESSERT	Mixed berry frozen yoghurt

What to do in advance

- Make the omelette (serve it as a cold dish)
- Prepare the risotto up to the point where you add the liquid
- Make the frozen yoghurt, keep it in the freezer

On the night

- Complete the risotto dish

the roast dinner

STARTER	Quick mushroom soup
MAIN COURSE	Roast chicken with all the trimmings
	Quick roasted vegetables
DESSERT	Easy chocolate mousse

What to do in advance

- Make the soup
- Make the chocolate mousse

On the night

- Reheat the soup
- Follow the timings for the roast dinner on page 68

the healthy option

MAIN COURSE   Thai fish cakes

Healthy chunky chips

DESSERT   Mixed berry frozen yoghurt

What to do in advance

- Make the fish cakes and chill
- Cut and microwave the potatoes
- Make the frozen yoghurt

On the night

- Cook the fish cakes
- Roast the chips

lunch for the parents

MAIN COURSE   Fish pie

DESSERT   Chocolate sandwich cake

What to do in advance

- Make the fish pie
- Make the cake

On the night:

- Reheat the pie (allowing enough time for it to be hot all the way through)
- Serve the cake with extra fresh cream and raspberries

glossary of terms

A brief a–z of terms I've used and a few you may hear bandied about in cookery programmes.

Al denté – an Italian term describing food that is cooked so that it is firm to the bite (ie, not over cooked and floppy).

Bake blind – the term for cooking pastry cases without a filling, just paper and baking weights to protect the pastry.

Bain-marie – a French term for a roasting tin or saucepan half filled with water, into or over which you place your cooking dish. It protects food from fierce heat.

Basting – to brush or spoon liquid fat or juices over foods being roasted, to encourage moistness during cooking.

Blanching – cooking vegetables or fruits by plunging briefly into boiling water, to pre-cook, or retain colour.

Boil – to heat liquid until it is a mass of quick moving bubbles.

Bouillon – another name for stock.

Bouquet garni – a small bundle of flavourings for soups and stews, usually thyme, rosemary, bay leaf.

Braising – baking or stewing meat, poultry or vegetables in liquid in a covered pot.

Brown – when cooking meat, this means cooking the outer edges of the meat (sealing) until it colours slightly.

Canapé – a French term for bite-sized appetisers served with drinks.

Caramelise – to allow the food cooking to turn to the colour and/or consistency of caramel.

Casserole – refers to both the ovenproof dish and the method of slow cooking in the oven.

Creaming – blending together butter and sugar, or a general mixing term to produce a smooth, cream coloured finish.

Croute – a bread disc usually fried used for carrying a topping.

Croutons – small fried cubes of bread used for garnishing soups and salads.

Crudities – sticks of raw vegetables for dipping into a thick sauce usually served as an appetiser.

Drizzle – to drip or slowly pour a small amount of liquid over or around some food.

Emulsify – to mix together two ingredients slowly and to form a smooth sauce such as mayonnaise.

En croute – wrapped in pastry.

En Papillote – food that is cooked in a bag of paper or foil.

Flambé – French for flaming. Certain foods are sprinkled with alcohol, which is ignited before serving.

Fold – to use a large metal spoon to incorporate one mixture into another very gently.

Fry – to heat oil or butter in a pan and cook food allowing it to colour.

Griddle – to cook using a griddle pan which is a heavy frying pan with ridges that scorch and pattern food.

Infuse – to mix ingredients with a liquid to impart their flavour, tea is an infusion.

Julienne – term for vegetables cut finely into strips.

Marinate – to place food into a seasoned liquid (a marinade) to absorb flavour or in some cases to tenderise.

Mirin – low alcohol, sweet golden wine used in Japanese cooking.

Par-boil – to part cook potatoes or other vegetables in water.

Poaching – to cook by simmering gently in a liquid.

Purée – liquidised, sieved or finely mashed fruit or vegetables.

Prove – putting aside dough or yeast batter to rise before baking.

Reduce – to boil a sauce or liquid to intensify flavour and reduce quantity.

Refresh – to place cooked vegetables into cold water after boiling to stop cooking and keep their colour.

Relax or
rest – to allow the pastry time in the fridge to settle, avoids shrinkage. Joints of roasted meats are left to 'rest', this allows time for the juices to settle and makes for easier carving.

Roux – flour and butter cooked gently in a pan as a base for a sauce or gravy.

Sauté – to fry quickly in hot fat.

Seasoned
flour – plain flour seasoned with salt and pepper.

Shredded – to finely cut into very thin ribbons. Used especially for vegetables.

Simmer – describes a liquid that is heated to a very gentle bubbling point.

Skillet – ridged frying pan, similar to a griddle pan.

Sweat – to cook vegetables very gently in a pan with butter, usually with a lid and with no colour on the vegetables.

Whipped – hand whisked or whisked by machine to incorporate air.

Zest – the skin of any citrus fruit, thinly peeled without the white pith.

weights & measures

It doesn't matter whether you work with metric or imperial measurements, just ensure you stick with one or the other throughout a recipe as the conversions are approximate. For further reference I've also included cup measurements that are favoured in the US.

liquid

Imperial		Metric
1 tsp		5 ml
1 tbsp		15 ml
5 tbsp		75 ml
$^1/_4$ pint	5 fl oz	150 ml
$^1/_2$ pint	10 fl oz	300 ml
$^3/_4$ pint	15 fl oz	425 ml
1 pint	20 fl oz	570 ml
1$^3/_4$ pint	35 fl oz	1000 ml/1 litre

oven temperatures

115°C	240°F	gas mark $^1/_4$
130°C	250°F	gas mark $^1/_2$
140°C	285°F	gas mark 1
150°C	300°F	gas mark 2
160°C	320°F	gas mark 3
180°C	350°F	gas mark 4
190°C	375°F	gas mark 5
200°C	400°F	gas mark 6
220°C	425°F	gas mark 7
235°C	450°F	gas mark 8

weight

Imperial	US	Metric
$^1/_4$ oz	1 tsp	7 g
$^1/_2$ oz	1 tbsp	15 g
1 oz	2 tsbp/ $^1/_8$ cup	30 g
(a heaped tablespoon of flour weighs about an ounce)		
2 oz	$^1/_4$ cup	55 g
3 oz	$^1/_3$ cup	85 g
4 oz/ $^1/_4$ lb	$^1/_2$ cup	110 g
5 oz	$^5/_8$ cup	140 g
6 oz	$^3/_4$ cup	170 g
7 oz	$^7/_8$ cup	200 g
8 oz/ $^1/_2$ lb	1 cup	225 g
9 oz	1$^1/_8$ cups	250 g
10 oz	1$^1/_4$ cups	285 g
12 oz/ $^3/_4$ lb	1$^1/_2$ cups	340 g
14 oz	1$^3/_4$ cups	400 g
16 oz/ 1lb	2 cups	450 g
$^1/_4$ lb	2$^1/_2$ cups	560 g
$^1/_2$ lb	3 cups	675 g
2 lb	4 cups	900 g
3 lb	6 cups	1.35 kg
4 lb	8 cups	1.8 kg
5 lb	10 cups	2.3 kg
6 lb	12 cups	2.7 kg

Note
Cup measurements are approximate and will vary according to the volume of your ingredients

happy cooking

This book is not just for men but really any beginner who wants to be a good home cook. Whether you're single and looking to impress, or attached and looking to treat and astonish your partner then this book is sure to help.

If you've yet to attempt any of the featured recipes and have merely flicked though the book let me assure you, as someone who spends a great deal of time cooking for other people, what a massive treat and delight it is to be cooked for once in a while, so don't delay that virgin voyage into the kitchen any longer. As your confidence and skills develop you're sure to discover that cooking is a marvellous way to relax. You'll find that the chopping, slicing, crushing and indeed all the processes which take you to eating will clear your mind from the stresses of the day.

So I wish you happy, healthy cooking and eating.

Above all enjoy it!

I would like to thank my Suffolk friends and their husbands who tested recipes for this book. And to Alistair, Tilly and Bobby for being my best guinea pigs and dearest family.

index